The Old Testament
in
Sociological Perspective

The
Old Testament
in
Sociological Perspective

A. D. H. Mayes

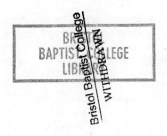

Marshall Pickering

Marshall Morgan and Scott
Marshall Pickering
34 – 42 Cleveland Street, London, W1P 5FB. U.K.

Acknowledgments

Beacon Press
  for quotations from Weber: *The Sociology of Religion*, copyright English
  translation 1963 by Beacon Press

Cambridge University Press
  for quotations from Giddens: *Capitalism and Modern Social Theory*

Oxford University Press
  for quotations from Weber: *Essays in Sociology*, trans. H. H. Gerth and
  C. Wright Mills; and *Karl Marx: Selected Writings*, ed. D. McLellan
  (1977)

SCM Press Ltd
  for quotations from Theissen: *Biblical Faith* (1984) (copyright holder in
  USA and Canada: Fortress Press); and Gottwald: *The Tribes of Yahweh*
  (1980) (copyright holder in USA and Canada: Orbis Books)

Sheffield Academic Press
  for quotations from Frick: *The Formation of the State in Ancient Israel*

Unwin Hyman Ltd
  for quotations from Durkheim: *The Elementary Forms of the Religious Life*;
  and from Weber: *The Protestant Ethic and the Spirit of Capitalism*

British Library CIP Data

Mayes, Andrew, 1945 –
  The Old Testament in sociological perspective.
  1. Bible O.T.
  I. Title
  221

  ISBN: 0 551 01937 9

Text Set in Baskerville by Avocet Robinson, Buckingham
Printed in Great Britain by Camelot Press Ltd, Shirley, Southampton

For Elizabeth

Contents

Foreword

If any justification were needed for this book it could be provided by words from the introduction: 'a (sociological) theory or perspective is indeed present, either explicitly or implicitly, in any account of Israel' (p. 3). This being so, it is essential that students of the Old Testament should have available to them text books that raise and inform their sociological awareness. There is, however, an additional factor which makes the present work especially timely, and that is the recent upsurge in research and writing on the sociology of the Old Testament. Although this work has shed much light on the origin and nature of Israelite society and prophecy, it has also raised some fundamental questions about the nature of the religion of the Old Testament. For example, approaches which stress material and economic factors in the constitution of societies, may appear to do less than justice to the understanding of Israel's faith and identity as expressed in the Old Testament.

Professor Mayes confronts this problem skilfully by contrasting the 'conflict tradition' in sociology (Weber and those who have used his insights for Old Testament study) with the 'structural-functionalist tradition' (Durkheim and those who have used his insights for Old Testament study). The result is an introduction to social theory, an account of its application to the Old Testament, including the most recent developments, and a conclusion which addresses the question of how to maintain a proper balance between emphasis on the non-human factors of society and the shaping which results, among other things, from religious awareness within society. This is an authoritative and well-balanced book which will guide students carefully through some of the major current questions of Old Testament history, society and religion.

Professor J. W. Rogerson, MA, DD

Preface

Although this book has been a number of years in the making, I am very much aware that it stands at the threshold of my exploration of exciting and promising developments in biblical studies. The sociological field is vast and somewhat daunting, but the rewards in terms of a fresh view of the Old Testament and ancient Israel fully justify the time and effort which it demands. I hope that this book will help to dispel some of the aura of impenetrable mystery with which the topic is sometimes surrounded, and encourage further and deeper study of the paths into Israel's society and faith which it opens up.

My acknowledgement of the help of colleagues is very much more than formal. Ronald Clements, by asking me to undertake the volume and providing comments and suggestions in the course of its writing, has placed me very much in his debt. John Rogerson favoured me with a detailed critique of an early plan of the work, and in doing so brought it much more into the mainstream of sociological studies of the Old Testament. My colleagues in Trinity College, Sean Freyne, John Bartlett and Werner Jeanrond, have provided a general critical sounding board from which, I hope, readers will benefit. I am especially grateful to Werner Jeanrond for reading and criticizing parts of the manuscript, and thereby helping me to clarify my thinking on quite unfamiliar themes.

I am glad to acknowledge once more the generous support of the Alexander von Humboldt Stiftung, which made possible a period of study at the University of Tübingen. The thoughtful hospitality there of Professor Martin Hengel created a congenial atmosphere for writing an earlier draft of this book.

A. D. H. Mayes
Trinity College
Dublin

Introduction

What possible relevance can sociology have to the study of the Old Testament and ancient Israel? If sociology is understood to be concerned with the collation of masses of empirical data, the discovery of opinions and trends by means of questionnaires, and the construction of hypotheses about the future on the basis of such study, then indeed its relevance to a society of which we have only very partial knowledge, and that from three thousand years ago, must surely be minimal (Rodd:1979, 467 ff.; 1981, 105). The information is simply not available to us in order to find out what people then thought, how they tended to act, what influences shaped their thinking and acting, the social developments and tendencies within which they lived. There seems, indeed, to be an essential difference between history and sociology: history is about the past, sociology is about the present and the future.

On the other hand, the founding fathers of sociology, major figures such as Weber and Durkheim, admitted no such distinction. Not only did they freely absorb history into the very fabric of their sociological studies, but one of them, Weber, wrote extensively and influentially on ancient Israel. Sociology, as they understood it, was intimately associated with history. More recently, a relationship between the two has been expressed in these terms: historical method and sociological method are complementary methods of approach to the study of ancient Israel, the one concerned with 'the sequential articulation of Israel's experience', and the other with the structure and function of patterns of relationship both at a given moment and 'in their trajectories of change' in history (Gottwald:1979,69; 1980,16f.; Yamauchi:1984, 176). This, however, seems an unrealistic distinction: the 'sequential articulation of Israel's experience' cannot be taken to exclude the 'trajectories of change' in the structure and function of her

1

internal relations. These two aspects of the study of ancient Israel belong together as social history; one of them cannot be isolated as sociology and the other as history.

The nature of sociology, or at least an essential characteristic of sociology, may be clarified by reference to Weber ([1919] 1948,135f.), who wrote that all calculations and observations involved in sociological study remain fruitless without 'ideas' which can give them direction. Such ideas cannot take the place of calculations; nor do they arise simply on the basis of calculations, but they come unexpectedly and in their own time.

Essential to sociology, therefore, is not simply the availability of unlimited data about society, even if sociological hypotheses comprehend, depend upon and are strengthened by such data. Rather, sociology requires both the data and the idea which organizes the data, the insight by which the otherwise mute data become intelligible. Past societies may yield less data than modern societies, but they are no less open to sociological understanding. Sociology is, therefore, a way of bringing together the insight arising from ideas and the facts yielded by observation (Nisbet:1967,5f.). It concerns itself with theorizing about the nature of society, creating models and hypotheses, perspectives through which the information, whether of the present or the past, may be given comprehensible order.

The ability to raise sociological questions seems to presuppose a certain detachment from society, a loosening of the social bonds, the possibility of standing outside and examining a society which is no longer implicitly accepted as unchanging and unchangeable. The nineteenth century offered the conditions for such thinking, to the extent that the period 1830–1910 has been described as the golden age of sociology. It is to this time that the great classics, the works of Marx, Weber and Durkheim, belong, writings to which more recent sociological study is still deeply indebted. Nisbet has identified two forces in particular as creating the conditions for the appearance of these works: the industrial revolution and the French revolution. The first involved urbanization, technology and the factory system, with the shift of property from land to capital, all of which signalled a break in traditional social structures; the French revolution was an ideological revolution which deliberately overturned traditional institutions and customs in the process of centralizing all authority

2

in the state. These forces dislocated the structural elements of society which had been fixed and stable since the Middle Ages. Sociology thus emerged in the nineteenth century as the theoretical search for new contexts within which to locate those typical characteristics of all societies; within sociological thinking there then developed theories on the nature of society and of social dynamics.

With reference to the study of Israel, then, it may be said that the sociological approach is concerned with the development of a social theory as the means by which an understanding of the nature of the ancient society of Israel in its ongoing history might be created. Such an approach recognizes that Israel is not to be understood simply by a search for the data, the brute facts, of its society or of its history; such facts can become intelligible to us, and so form an account of Israel, only within the context of a theory about, a perspective on, society. Such a theory or perspective is indeed present, either explicitly or implicitly, in any account of Israel; the sociological approach consciously articulates that theory or perspective. What, it asks, is the most appropriate understanding of the nature of society within which and through which it is possible to comprehend what the Old Testament and archaeology tell us of ancient Israel? There are different theories on the nature of society; there are different comprehensions of Israel. Sociology is concerned with such theories and the foundations on which they rest. The sociological approach to ancient Israel is, then, largely concerned with the theoretical perspective presupposed in the study of ancient Israelite history and society. This perspective and the different forms which it has taken in recent Old Testament study is the subject of this book.[1]

1

Early Sociological Theory and Recent Old Testament Study

Introduction

If sociology in this context is concerned with the perspective on society, the theory about society, through which the data of Israelite history, society and religion are perceived and understood, it is surely the case that any work on Israelite history, society or religion is sociological, either by implication or design. Sociological concerns need not be an explicit factor in a work in order that perspectives properly classified as sociological should form a significant, indeed the necessary, element in its construction. How, then, may a review of sociological perspectives on the Old Testament and ancient Israel, explicit or implicit, be organized? It would be possible to proceed in a straightforward chronological or biographical fashion, describing the sociological ideas behind major contributions to the study of Israelite history, society and religion. This style of approach, concentrating on explicitly sociological studies, does appear in a number of works (Hahn:1966; Kraus:1972; Schottroff:1974,1982; Thiel:1983), but it is in some respects unsatisfactory: it is not sufficiently analytical, in the sense of setting such studies within the framework of general sociological theory, nor is it systematic enough to supply a sociological theory or set of theories which may be used to uncover the implicit sociological ideas in those works which such reviews omit to analyse.

It would be possible, on the other hand, to identify typically sociological themes and investigate their place in Old Testament study. This systematic approach has been applied most successfully by Nisbet within the context of general sociology. Five themes have been isolated by him as constitutive for sociology: community, authority, status, the sacred, and alienation. These themes appear in the major works of the golden age of sociology, and it is a basic concern with them which effectively distinguishes the sociological from other disciplines. If this approach were to be transposed to the present context, our procedure would be to examine the way in which a sociological understanding of these themes lies behind various historical, social and religious studies of ancient Israel. This approach, however, fruitful as it would be, carries the dangers of a loss of historical perspective and of a tendency to oversystematize. Indeed, a criticism of Nisbet's work, which is closely relevant to Old Testament study, is that he has tended to blur the distinction between Durkheim's presentation of the sacred and Weber's understanding of charisma and its routinization, in order to discuss both as treatments of one sociological theme. Nevertheless, Nisbet has provided a fully examined classification of what must be topical constants within the area of sociology and the Old Testament.

A middle path (adopted by Malina:1982) is to distinguish at least two sociological traditions, the conflict tradition and the structural-functionalist tradition, or, to use the names of their respective major or founding representatives, the Weber tradition and the Durkheim tradition; and, having defined their distinctive and distinguishing theories on society, to attempt a classification of sociological approaches to the Old Testament within the categories which they provide. This approach is systematic enough to allow for the development of a general sociological system of classification, which may be applied also outside the necessarily limited range of materials to be covered here; it is also flexible enough to allow for the comprehension of real differences in the understanding of the nature of society presupposed by different authors.

Much of the present work follows this middle path, either by incorporating studies of the Old Testament and ancient Israel within one or other of these sociological traditions, or by expressing a critique of such studies from the perspective of these traditions. The two traditions should not be isolated in any absolute way, for there are many respects in which they overlap and interact, and, indeed, it is not always easy to see into which tradition any given work should be placed. It will, furthermore,

6

be suggested in the concluding chapter that the direction in which some recent sociological theory points, and which promises the most convincing contribution to our understanding of Israelite history, society and religion, is one which brings essential aspects of both traditions into an interacting relationship.

The rise of sociological theory in the nineteenth century

Despite the distinctiveness which the Weber and Durkheim sociological traditions came to exhibit, they have a common root in nineteenth century sociological theory. For their understanding of the nature of society, both conflict and structural-functionalist traditions depend on the work of Tönnies, and in their understanding of religion they both reflect a rejection of the adequacy of the positivist view that religion is but primitive science. This common root should not be too quickly neglected in the interests of showing its development into its later two shoots, for there is significant recent work on ancient Israel which may be directly traced back to it, and especially to the sociological theory of Tönnies.

Tönnies wrote a social history of western Europe in its transition from medievalism to modernism, which he described as a transition from 'community' (*Gemeinschaft*) to 'society' (*Gesellschaft*). These terms at first had direct historical reference, but Tönnies also understood them to denote theoretical types of social structure rather than empirical historical forms. The distinction between empirical historical form, on the one hand, and type, on the other, is a crucial one which will appear repeatedly as basic to sociological study: the empirical historical form is an actual concrete structure belonging to a particular time and place; the type is a theoretical model, a deliberately articulated theoretical construction, which is essential in order to comprehend and to classify the particular historical form. As types, community and society are models through which the social structure and history of any people in any period may be illuminated. The types are theoretical constructs which never exist empirically in pure form, but may be used as heuristic models in order to illuminate fundamental characteristics of any given historical situation.

Tönnies described the type of community as an intimate and exclusive social group. Its prototype is the family, in which are found in purest form the characteristics of unity which are fundamental to it. It is a basic and original condition of human life and exists quite apart from and independent of any rational or economic decision. Community is not, however, confined to the limits of the family; it is found also as a social form based on common habitat (*Gemeinschaft* of locality) or even on common intellectual interests (*Gemeinschaft* of mind).

The type of society, on the other hand, is the structure characteristic of European civilization in its modern form. It is no longer a community of kinship, locality or mind, but has become a complex network of legal and moral relations. A society is essentially rational in its foundation. It

> . . . superficially resembles the Gemeinschaft in so far as the individuals live and dwell together peacefully. However, in the Gemeinschaft they remain essentially united in spite of all separating factors, whereas in the Gesellschaft they are essentially separated in spite of all uniting factors. In the Gesellschaft, as contrasted with the Gemeinschaft, we find no actions that can be derived from an a priori and necessarily existing unity; no actions, therefore, which manifest the will and the spirit of the unity even if performed by the individual; no actions which, in so far as they are performed by the individual, take place on behalf of those united with him . . . On the contrary, here everybody is by himself and isolated, and there exists a condition of tension against all others . . . nobody wants to grant and produce anything for another individual . . . if it be not in exchange for a gift or labor equivalent that he considers at least equal to what he has given (Tönnies: [1887]1963,64f.).

In the *Gesellschaft* the relationship of individuals to material objects has priority. In the *Gemeinschaft* the relationship to material objects is secondary to the mutual relations of the members of the community among themselves; material objects are usually used and possessed in common.

This social theory considerably influenced the thinking of Weber and Durkheim. Weber's distinction ([1921] 1947,136ff.) between communal and associative relationships closely corresponds to that between *Gemeinschaft* and *Gesellschaft*. A relationship is communal when it 'is based on a subjective feeling of the parties . . . that they belong together'. Such relationships may be found in 'a religious brotherhood, an erotic relationship, a relation of personal loyalty, a national community, the *esprit de corps* of a military unit', but they are 'most conveniently illustrated by the family'. An associative relationship, on the other hand, usually rests on a rational agreement by mutual consent; as a voluntary association of individuals, free of emotional identification, it finds its purest form in such relationships as the rational free market exchange.

Even at this basic level, however, Weber significantly modified the social theory he derived from Tönnies. Whereas Tönnies used the terms *Gemeinschaft* and *Gesellschaft*, Weber introduced the terms *Vergemeinschaftung* and *Vergesellschaftung* (the making of community, the making of society). This indicates that for Weber what was sociologically significant was action which creates a social relationship rather than the relationship in itself. An emphasis on the primacy for sociology of the understandable actions of individuals, with the implication that communal and associative relationships are secondary and dependent formations, is of fundamental importance for the sociological tradition rooted in Weber. This will be developed further at a later stage; for the present, it may be noted that Weber followed Tönnies in treating these forms as theoretical types rather than as particular historical examples. On the empirical, historical level, aspects of both types may be discovered in any one social structure; moreover, the communal does not necessarily have priority over the associative relationship. An associative relationship, based on contract, may, if it endure long enough, form the basis for an emerging communal relationship; on the other hand, the communal relationship, even the family, may be the setting within which relationships come to be governed by self-interest of an associative kind. Generally, however, Weber, like Tönnies, understood the process of change to be from the communal to the associative relationship, a process which Weber termed 'rationalization'.[1]

Durkheim (1933) made a similar distinction between societies characterized by what he termed mechanical solidarity and those characterized by organic solidarity. In a society of the former type, individuals scarcely differ from one another: they are members of the same collectivity and resemble one another because they feel the same emotions, cherish the same values,

9

hold the same things sacred and own property in common. There is as yet no differentiation. Such societies have a segmentary structure: they consist of similar, juxtaposed clan groups. The whole is a cultural unity. On the other hand, a society characterized by organic solidarity is one in which differentiation has taken place. Social order rests now on the complementarity of individuals who are free of the traditional restraints exercised by kinship, locality, and the generalized social conscience. The unity of society is no longer a cultural unity embracing beliefs, values and property, but is the unity of free and independent individuals who complement one another within the larger whole by their differences rather than their similarities.

On religion, Weber and Durkheim held views which reflected in part a common rejection of religious positivism. Positivism, as expressed particularly in the work of the founder of sociology, Auguste Comte, treated religion and magic as primitive science, an outlook and practice destined to succumb to the advance of scientific knowledge; as rational, scientific knowledge develops, so the magical and religious ideas which it replaces become irrelevant and disappear. For both Weber and Durkheim, on the other hand, religion and rationality represent different forms of understanding which exist alongside each other; they have different concerns and relate to different issues and questions (see Parsons:1944).

Weber argued that a distinction is to be drawn between problems of empirical causation and problems of meaning, in so far as these are significant for human actions. In such cases as premature death the problem of *how* it happened, in the sense of empirical cause, can readily be solved, but yet leave a sense of both emotional and cognitive frustration as to *why* it happened. Religion is concerned with the latter, and it is with respect to their treatment of such problems of meaning that the great religious systems are primarily distinguished. For Durkheim, too, the realm of the sacred is wholly different from that of the profane, and the beliefs attaching to these realms must be understood to represent two quite separate systems. Durkheim considered ceremonies associated with death as a social mechanism for re-establishing the solidarity of the group on the occasion of severe strain and disruption. Whatever the differences and contrasts between the more developed views of Weber and Durkheim, they at least had this in common, that they perceived religion as a system of beliefs and practices which could not be reduced to the positivist level of primitive science.

The influence of early sociological theory on recent Old Testament study

The typological distinction between *Gemeinschaft* and *Gesellschaft* has proved to be extraordinarily influential in Old Testament studies. A pioneer in the sociological approach, whose work echoes that distinction, was L. Wallis (1912; 1935; 1942; cf. May: 1944; Sasson: 1981,11f.). Israelite history was described by him as a struggle between the original nomadic life style of Israelite clans and the urban society of Canaanites, between a social system characterized by brotherhood and lack of private property, on the one hand, and one characterized by a class system based on property ownership, on the other. The egalitarian ethic of the clan could not be the dominant force in the new sedentary culture, but the conflict between the two, coming to expression in the creative prophetic opposition to the class system, gave rise to an understanding of social justice and of the nature of Yahweh which at least secured his independence from the class and property interests of civilized society.

Both issues, the distinction between *Gemeinschaft* and *Gesellschaft*, and Yahweh's independence from social interests, are fundamental to the views of Mendenhall (1973, 1–31, 174–97; 1975, 169–80; 1976, 132–51). His basic argument is that the origins of Israel marked a decisive break with the past, as a result of which religion became the foundation for social unity expressed through the instrument of the covenant. The revolution occurred in the formation of a new community at Sinai. Whereas in primitive tribalism religion was the ritualistic means of maintaining the solidarity of the group and of influencing the supernatural world to give the group what it wished, with the emergence of Israel religion became man's voluntary submission to the will of God defined in ethical terms. Religion, having formerly been an expression of the interests of the social group, became, with the foundation of Israel, the basis of the group's existence. It was in its formative years that Israel was radically distinct from the political state: early Israel was the kingdom of Yahweh, a value system in which a community realized in its daily life values which are personal rather than economic or corporate. The introduction of the monarchy, however, represented a reassimilation on the part of Israel to Late Bronze Age religious ideas and structures, in which religion was politicized. The state is a power structure, a system of social control. The contrast between the early community of Israel and the monarchic state of Israel can also be expressed as one between covenant and law. Covenant is the foundation of a community of individuals who voluntarily accept its obligations; it is not under the control of any social organization nor does it require any social control system for its existence. Law is an instrument of control within a social order; it depends on fear and authoritarian enforcement; it tends to become formal and devoid of ethical content; it requires social institutions for its existence and realization. The state (law) benefits from covenant community, but it cannot produce it or control it; covenant community affirms the reality of the transcendent in human life and experience, and effectively rejects social power as ultimate authority. For Mendenhall, early Israel is a *Gemeinschaft* while the monarchic state is a *Gesellschaft*; these represent the foundational categories through which Israel is to be understood, and her history is a development from the former to the latter.

Mendenhall's understanding of Israel has been adopted and developed by Herion (1981). Different literary expressions in the Old Testament (of which Micah 6:1–5 and Psalm 105 are taken as representative) are argued by Herion to reflect alternative world views and epistemologies, and these are to be derived from distinct social contexts which may be described in typological terms. Using the sociological model of the folk-urban continuum, Herion has described the one social context as folk, characterized by personal and traditional relationships, no division of labour and cultural community and solidarity, and the other as urban, characterized by impersonal and transitory social relations, differentiation of labour and cultural heterogeneity.

Folk community treats individuals as valuable in and for themselves, and is founded on the internalization of traditional values and norms to which it constantly seeks to adapt itself, rather than on the external compulsion of law; urban society requires a formal and deliberately created social structure marked by law and force, and a mythical form of historiography which is not bound by tradition but alters the past to make it conform to and legitimize the present. It was the experience of the collapse of (urban) social control systems which led many in Palestine to reject political force and to adopt more folklike internalized values of self-control rooted in the covenant or treaty structure of society. The rise of the Israelite monarchic state, however, reintroduced the urban social control system, and created tension between the two social patterns. The folk tendency, typical of deprived elements of society, challenged the urban, using the traditional past to critique the mythical sacrosanctity of the present advocated by the urban; it indeed also influenced the urban sector, at least in so far as official urban historiography uses the form of relating history, a form rooted in the covenant, as a way of legitimizing present institutions. In this presentation, *Gemeinschaft* and *Gesellschaft* are treated as types which, while in general standing in that order of chronological priority, are also understood to interact in a complex way within the one social structure whose diversity may be comprehended by the model of the folk-urban continuum.

The contrast which Dietrich (1979) has developed between Israelite and Canaanite in the monarchic period expresses very similar sociological ideas. Israelite and Canaanite are described as two very different cultures: the former characterized by social equality, little specialization in labour and property held in common, and the latter by strict social classification, hierarchy, division of labour and concentration of wealth. David attempted to integrate the Canaanite city state social system into the Israelite national system by allowing each cultural sector a representative role within his administration, but his policy was not successful; at the end of his reign there were two opposed parties, the Israelite led by Adonijah, and the Canaanite led by Solomon. Solomon's victory resulted in the promotion of city state interests, but in opposition there eventually developed the nationalistic reaction which brought Jeroboam to the throne in Israel. The subsequent royal history of both Israel and Judah may, at least at first, be interpreted within the framework of the polarity between Israelite and

13

Canaanite (see also Andersen: 1966; Rohrbaugh: 1978, 55ff.). Zimri favoured the Canaanite faction in reaction to the middle path which Baasha and Elah had attempted to follow, while the Omride policy of compromise was ruined by the extreme Israelite attitudes of Jehu. By the time of Jeroboam II, however, a development had taken place in which Israel had become Canaanized, the old dualism overshadowed by a new one between an upper class and a lower class. This change, which is reflected in the social criticism of the prophets, involved an ever greater accumulation of capital in the hands of a few, and impoverishment and loss of independence on the part of the general population. The history of the southern kingdom shows a parallel tension between Israelite and Canaanite, rural and urban interests. Here, however, the later economic division in the population did not at first replace the traditional dualism: both Hezekiah and Josiah represented the interests of the nationalistic anti-Canaanite party. Subsequently, however, the imposition of taxation in order to raise tribute for Egypt created economic division within the Israelite party and so brought the traditional cultural distinctions to an end.

The sociological categories used in the studies of apocalyptic by Plöger (1968) and Hanson (1979) are of a similar nature. Apocalyptic is the means by which eschatologically oriented communities or conventicles, comparable to sects, express their identity and self-understanding. The apocalyptic movement is a *Gemeinschaft* alienated from the theocratic establishment: the members of the community are separated from the normative socio-religious structure, have no part in its institutional arrangements and do not share its religious world view. The apocalyptic community constructs an alternative symbolic universe, characterized by visionary expectation of the intervention of God into the present to effect its deliverance, salvation and vindication. It expresses this expectation through apocalyptic eschatology: this is a radical transformation of prophetic eschatology, which has broken the ties with history which prophetic eschatology had carefully maintained. The background of this transformation lies in the exile and restoration, for these events led to a religious and social division between the returned Zadokites, who seized control and leadership, and those who had remained in Palestine during the exile and now, deprived of their rightful position, were excluded from influence and power. It is within this latter group that apocalyptic

14

eschatology was fostered as a response to deprivation. The contrast between the two social groups is reflected in, for example, the contrast between the pragmatic restoration programme of Ezekiel 40–48 and the visionary programme of Isaiah 60–62. For the adherents to the visionary programme the present political and social order is beyond redemption; through divine action, described by means of the traditional divine warrior motif, it will be destroyed. This is a conflict between a church, on the one hand, regarded as being compromised with the world, co-extensive with society, rationalized and formalized, and a sect, on the other hand, a primary social group, a *Gemeinschaft*, which rejects the values of the dominant society and maintains the original pure faith. The conflict comes to literary expression in the contrast between ideology, which justifies the status quo, and utopia, which is a vision of transformation.

Brueggemann's study (1979) of two trajectories which he claims to be able to trace through the Old Testament and the social history of Israel is effectively a summary statement of an approach to the Old Testament and ancient Israel on this sociological basis[2]. On the one hand, there is the Mosaic covenant trajectory, the theology of the 'have-nots', rooted in the pre-monarchic Israelite tribal community, which emerged as an alternative society to the city-state culture, and continued as a revolutionary movement in the northern kingdom through to the post-exilic period; on the other hand, there is the Davidic covenant trajectory, which embraced the imperial myths of the ancient Near East, and had a comprehensive world view, promoting social stability rather than social transformation and liberation.

Clearly the *Gemeinschaft-Gesellschaft* typology has been enormously influential in defining the framework within which Israelite history and its reflection in Old Testament texts have been explored. It has formed the sociological perspective, the understanding of the form which society takes, through which the historical, social and religious data relating to ancient Israel have been comprehended and ordered. To a greater or lesser degree, however, unresolved sociological problems are to be found in these studies. First, the nature of the sociological categories which are presupposed is not always clearly defined. Tönnies defined the *Gemeinschaft* and the *Gesellschaft* as two types of society, rather than as two empirical social structures. The

15

descriptions of Israelite society appearing in many of the works noted above, however, and perhaps especially in the studies of Mendenhall and Hanson, apparently presuppose these categories as descriptions of actually existing social structures: the nature and function of the type in its relationship to the empirical social structure have been neglected. Herion, it is true, is careful to argue that the folk and the urban are types which belong on a continuum; but in so far as so much significant material in the Old Testament (as, for example, Deuteronomy) is held by him to represent cross-fertilization between the types, then the usefulness or appropriateness of the types for the Israelite context at least must be open to question (see further Brett: 1987).

Secondly, early Israelite society is reconstructed in a way that is open to the charge of idealism. This is especially so of Mendenhall's and Herion's view of the early Israelite *Gemeinschaft* as a social structure dependent upon internalized values and constructed as an alternative to the power systems of social control. The origins of Israel have been divorced from the normal range of social, economic and historical influences in the interests of presenting an original Israelite community (*Gemeinschaft*) as an empirical reality utterly different from other social structures, particularly the state. The contribution of socio-economic, environmental and other factors, however, to the formation of early Israel cannot be set aside in the quest for a comprehensive understanding, even if such factors tend to blur the historical and sociological distinctiveness with which early Israel may be described.

Thirdly, the relationship between the social context in historical Israel and the literary forms which appear in the Old Testament is simply assumed to be that the latter immediately and directly reflect the former. As Kovacs (1976) has noted in his discussion of Hanson's work, however, a range of alternative possibilities exists here: so, it could be argued that apocalypticism is not the direct reflection of the deprivations suffered by a *Gemeinschaft*, but rather arose as a compensation for the destabilizing of society caused by the exile and later Hellenization, in which case it would have served to reintroduce stability into the whole social system by drawing off the resentments of the disaffected; or, in the framework of a differentiated society, it may be that apocalyptic eschatology is an ideology quite incongruent with the social status of those who adhered to it, since people can and do hold belief systems inconsistent with their place in society; or, one might argue that since it is those who have some access to the rewards of social influence and power, and thus see what is possible, who really feel deprived, apocalyptic should be seen as deriving from much closer to the centre of society than Hanson allows; or, on the basis that the 'manifest' or apparent function of apocalyptic may be very different from its 'latent' or hidden function, it could be argued that apocalypticism served, paradoxically, to confirm the situation of the social élites by devaluing their successful participation in the dominant culture; or, given that apocalyptic now appears as literature in which its thought is systematically expressed, it could be argued that it no longer partakes of the *ad hoc* nature of the ideology of a movement which seeks change, but reflects rather the movement's reordering of its value system in order to become more accommodating to the dominant society.[3] This range of sociological possibilities indicates the need for a more aware understanding of the nature of sociological models and perspectives and their relationship both to history and to literature.

An Outline of Classical Sociology

The criticisms noted at the end of the last chapter have much wider application than to those approaches to the Old Testament which reflect the sociological theory of Tönnies. The place of idealism and materialism in historical reconstruction and the understanding of religion in its relationship to society, the nature of ideology and its relation to social context, the nature of the type and its relationship with empirical reality, are all general sociological problems. These are issues which have become prominent in the development of sociological theory, and consequently arise also with regard to sociological presuppositions in the study of the Old Testament and ancient Israel. It is largely within the framework of two emergent sociological traditions, the conflict and the structural-functionalist traditions, that many of these issues come to the fore. Before extending our review of sociological factors at work in Old Testament study, it is necessary, therefore, to trace the main features of this developing sociological theory. This will be done by reference to the work of the two sociologists most relevant to this context, Weber and Durkheim.

The conflict tradition

The sociology of Max Weber

The conflict tradition, in which Weber's sociology stands, is the tradition to which Marx also belonged, and in fact Weber owed much of his substantive sociology to Marx. It is from Marx that he derived the view that values and ideas, though not merely derivative of material interests, must be analysed in relation to such interests (Giddens:1977,183–207; id.:1971,21ff.). This is of some importance in our present context, for too often Weber has been interpreted within the framework of a rather naïve contrast between him and Marx, according to which the latter was a materialist while Weber was an idealist. Thus, Weber's study of the relationship between capitalism and Calvinistic Protestantism has been widely understood as an idealistic refutation of Marxist historical materialism. This will be discussed in more detail shortly; for the moment, it may be stated to be a crude interpretation of both Weber and Marx, which distorts the role which both of them assigned to material and ideal interests in social formation.

The conflict tradition is so called because it understands society and social order to consist of individuals or groups in either violent or non-violent struggle to promote their own interests (Collins:1985,47). A structure of dominant and subordinate interest groups is the normal structure of society. Marx argued that capitalist society comprises two classes, the bourgeoisie and the proletariat, and that the struggle between them is a constitutive element of the historical process. The bourgeoisie is itself a revolutionary force, which brought to an end all feudal forms of relationship – kinship, religion, professional or personal relationship – and substituted an economic relationship. Under its rule, however, the proletariat is developing into a revolutionary force which will turn Europe in the future into a socialist, classless society (Marx:[1848]1977,222).

Both Marx and Weber were concerned with the analysis of modern capitalist society. While Marx, however, was chiefly interested in the economic basis of capitalism and its future breakdown, which he set within the framework of an inevitable historical process over which individuals have no control, Weber had a more historical interest in the rise of capitalism, and throughout his analysis he emphasized the subjective meanings, intentions and interpretations through which the individuals comprising a social group create and maintain it. An adequate social understanding, in Weber's view, always incorporates this subjective dimension: sociology is a science concerned with the subjective meanings and interpretations of social actors in the search for a causal explanation of events and situations (cf.Giddens:1971,146). Thus, the structures of society derive from the understandable actions of individuals who are to be seen as agents.

Weber's analysis of western civilization makes a basic distinction between society, on the one hand, and government or authority, on the other: society is not just the object of government, nor is government simply the outgrowth or byproduct of society. Societies are held together by the coalescence of the material and ideal interests of its constituent groups, together with the actions of governments ruling through bureaucracies. So Weber analysed society, on the one hand, and forms of rule or domination, on the other.

In his study of society, Weber took over much from Marx, but he adapted and supplemented Marxist analysis in one respect of major relevance to the present context: the term 'class', which in Marx has a broad and comprehensive economic, political and cultural sense, appears in Weber with application only to economic groups; other types of social group, without an economic foundation and therefore different from classes, also exist. The term which Weber used to designate a group formation which was not primarily economic was 'status group'. The status group comprises people of property and those without property; it is characterized by a particular life style and by restrictions, especially in marriage, in contact between those who are in and those outside the group. At its most extreme, in cases where ethnic distinctions are also held to be operative, the status group becomes a closed caste.

Such a caste situation is part of the phenomenon of 'pariah' peoples and is found all over the world. These peoples form communities, acquire specific occupational traditions of handicrafts or of other arts, and cultivate a belief in their ethnic community. They live in a 'diaspora' strictly segregated from all personal intercourse, except that of an unavoidable sort, and their situation is legally precarious. Yet, by virtue of their economic indispensability, they are tolerated, indeed, frequently privileged, and they live in interspersed political communities. The Jews are the most impressive historical example (Weber:[1913ff.]1948,189; see also Bendix:1960,86f.)

In his analysis of the nature of rule or authority, Weber ([1921]1968,215ff.) argued that authority is not simply the power to impose one's will, but is rather a relationship of dominance and subservience characterized by some measure of agreement

20

and compliance; it is not simply imposed but is accepted, and behind this acceptance there lies the recognition that it is legitimate. The claim to legitimacy, however, is not in every instance the same, and as it varies so also does the whole relationship and the means by which it is ordered. So, Weber distinguished three types of legitimate domination: legal authority, traditional authority and charismatic authority.

The person who exercises legal authority is also subject to law, and he is obeyed not as an individual but as the holder of an office. Legal authority is part of a total system characterized by a hierarchical organization of offices. Those who occupy offices within the system have demonstrated their eligibility through adequate technical training. It is a rationalized system or structure which may be found in very different contexts, in business, political or religious organizations (*ibid.*,221). It is determined by the needs of the time and by the particular values held by society at any given period; it belongs within the context of an 'association' rather than that of a 'community'.

Authority is traditional if it is based on acknowledged rules sanctified by antiquity (*ibid.*,226). This form of authority is based on personal loyalty; the person who exercises authority is not a superior aided by officials but a personal master assisted by his personal retainers. Here there is no rational hierarchy of offices, no technical training or clearly defined spheres of competence subject to impersonal rules. The demands of the traditional ruler are obeyed because their content is determined by the tradition, or, where this is not the case, because the personal loyalty due to him gives him a certain degree of discretion.

Charismatic authority relates to that quality of an individual who is considered to be gifted with powers which are recognized as exceptional and extraordinary or even of divine origin (*ibid.*,241). An organized group subject to charismatic authority is a charismatic community, in which there are no officials, no technical skills. This is an emotional form of communal relationship: the prophet and his disciples, the warlord and his bodyguard, to which there is no appointment, within which there is no career, no promotion, and from which there is no dismissal. Again, it is the contrast with other forms of authority which expresses the essence of charismatic authority. As an extraordinary, irrational form, charismatic authority stands sharply opposed to both legal and traditional authority: legal authority presupposes a rational system of rules, but charismatic authority is irrational in the sense of being outside all rules; traditional authority is bound by precedent, but charismatic authority is a revolutionary force which rejects the past (*ibid.*, 264).

These forms of authority are ideal types, and none of them is usually found historically in pure form. They may be related (see Weber:[1915]1948,295ff.) in that, through a process of 'routinization', charismatic authority may develop into traditional or even legal authority: rules emerge, which come to take the form of tradition, and in time offices and bureaucracies appear. Moreover (Weber:[1921]1968,263), the belief in legitimacy which is basic to all authority is usually complex: legal authority may well require a traditional or even a charismatic element for it to endure. Nevertheless, it is useful to analyse particular empirical examples from the perspective of the pure type in order to discern the dominant tendency and the internal dynamics of any given situation.

Authority is exercised through law, and so there are, corresponding to the different types of authority, different types of law or law-making. Here also Weber used an ideal type approach, and argued that there are different ways in which law is formed, which may be seen as different stages of development in an increasingly rational process of legal formulation. Again, it should be emphasized that these modes of law making, along with the scheme of development from one mode to another, are ideal type constructions, which cannot be immediately transposed into history; concrete cases of law making may exhibit two or more of these modes.

At first there is charismatic, or 'formally irrational', law making, which uses means outside the control of the intellect, particularly in so far as it involves the consultation of oracles. A second stage is the empirical creation of law by socially eminent individuals, or 'substantively irrational' law making; this is *ad hoc* decision making without public verifiable norms being brought to bear. A third stage is the imposition and systematization of laws by secular or theocratic powers, which is 'substantively rational' law making; this involves the application of existing collections of rules and norms to particular cases. Finally, there is the systematic and theoretical elaboration of laws by trained jurists, which is 'formally rational' law making; this relates to the formulation of highly abstract rules within the context of study, definition and exegesis in the law schools. The first two of these modes correspond to and belong within the context of charismatic and traditional forms of authority, respectively; the third and fourth are the procedures typical of legal authority.

Religion and society in Weber's sociology
Weber believed that religion is present in every human society; all societies conceive of a spiritual world which gives meaning to the unusual and rationally impenetrable aspects of experience (Weber:[1922]1965). There are two major types of religion, characterized by radically different attitudes towards the world: the inner-worldly attitude and the world-rejecting attitude. This distinction is, broadly, that between asceticism and mysticism, between occidental and oriental religion. Inner-worldly asceticism implies belief in a transcendent, omnipotent God who created the world out of nothing; salvation can be achieved not by mystical union with the divine but only through ethical justification before God through active conduct in the world. This is a religious attitude, expressed in a rational, methodical and unemotional approach to life and behaviour, found especially in ascetic Protestantism with its emphasis on the necessity for loyal fulfilment of obligations. In oriental mysticism, on the other hand, the world is not an object of divine creative activity, but is 'something simply presented to man, something which has been in the nature of things from all eternity', and so is 'a possible object of absolute rejection' (Weber:*ibid.*,178f.). The world-rejecting mystic rejects action in the world as a temptation against which he must maintain his state of grace; his aim is to achieve union with the divine through inactivity and contemplation.

In general terms, Weber related these distinct religious forms in a quite materialist way to particular forms of society: so, the personal, transcendent and ethical God of the Near East 'corresponds so closely to (the concept) of an all-powerful mundane king with his rational bureaucratic regime that a causal connection can scarcely be overlooked' (*ibid.*,56). The discussion of this aspect of Weber's sociology has, however, generally centred on his particular study of Protestantism ([1904–5]1976), and from this a quite different conclusion on Weber's view of religion and society has often been drawn. This study, it has been widely supposed, was intended by Weber as a refutation of the Marxist materialist view that religion is the ideological superstructure to given social conditions. Weber argued that modern capitalism, which is characterized by 'the earning of more and more money, combined with the strict avoidance of all spontaneous enjoyment of life' (*ibid.*,53), is to be understood within the framework of Calvinistic Protestantism. The three major tenets of this faith: that the universe is created to further the greater glory of God, that the motives of God are beyond human comprehension, and that eternal grace is predestined for the few from the beginning, offered no means of achieving salvation, but exposed the Calvinist to enormous strain and inner loneliness. Intense worldly activity and success were the means of countering this and developing and maintaining confidence that one is among the chosen; the performance of good works and success in a calling came to be regarded as a sign of election, so eliminating doubts about salvation. Thus, it has been argued, for Weber, the social phenomenon of capitalism is based on and derives from the religious ideas of ascetic Protestantism.

To describe Marx as a materialist and Weber as an idealist in this way is, however, a gross over-simplification. It is a vulgar form of Marxism which proposes that Marx believed that ideas play no part in history, that only material and technological forces are effective, and that history moves by the unconscious operation of its own laws, so that ideas become merely 'epiphenomena', the reflection of social and economic realities. For Marx, it was, in fact, only in the earliest stages of social development that human consciousness was the direct outcome of material activity, a mere herd consciousness.[1] 'The production of ideas, of conceptions, of consciousness, is at first directly interwoven with the material activity and the material intercourse of men, the language of real life. Conceiving, thinking, the mental intercourse of men, appear at this stage as the direct efflux of their material behaviour' (Marx:[1932]1977,164). With the development of society, however, particularly the expansion of social differentiation, 'consciousness is in a position to emancipate itself from the world and to proceed to the formation of "pure" theory, theology, philosophy, ethics, etc.' (*ibid.*,168; cf.Giddens:1971, 208f.). So a dialectical relationship is established, in which ideas, produced by human beings rooted in the material world, take on an independence of this root and act in a causative and creative way back upon society.

On the other hand, the idealist interpretation of Weber's work is equally distorting of his thought. At one point (1976,91), he noted that it was not his intention to maintain 'such a foolish and doctrinaire thesis as that the spirit of capitalism . . . could only have arisen as the result of certain effects of the Reformation . . . On the contrary, we only wish to ascertain whether and to what extent religious forces have taken part in the qualitative formation and quantitative expansion of that spirit over the world'; and later (*ibid.*,183), having discussed the contribution of ascetic Protestantism to the formation of capitalism, he wrote: 'it would also further be necessary to investigate how Protestant Asceticism was in turn influenced in its development and its character by the totality of social conditions, especially economic', and concluded by reaffirming that 'it is, of course, not my aim to substitute for a one-sided materialistic an equally one-sided spiritualistic causal interpretation of culture and of history'. In fact, Weber did not develop a systematic explanation of the relationship between ideas and material conditions as an alternative to either materialism or idealism (Bendix:1960,46f.).

On the specific issue of the social context of religious ideas, Weber did, however, argue (1965,80ff.) that neither peasants nor nobility ever appear as the carriers of rational, ethical movements. The lot of the peasant is so strongly tied to nature that as a rule the peasantry are chiefly involved with weather magic and animistic magic or ritualism. For the nobility, on the other hand, concepts like sin, salvation and religious humility are alien if not reprehensible to their sense of honour. With élite social classes religion functions primarily to legitimate their priviliged life pattern and situation in the world. It is, rather, the middle class which

> by virtue of its distinctive pattern of economic life, inclines in the direction of a rational, ethical religion, wherever conditions are present for the emergence of a rational, ethical religion . . . Furthermore, the artisan and in certain circumstances even the merchant lead economic existences which influence them to entertain the view that honesty is the best policy, that faithful work in the performance of obligations

will find their reward and are 'deserving' of their just compensation (*ibid.*,97).

The term which Weber used occasionally to describe the relationship between (religious) ideas and social conditions was 'elective affinity' (1948,62f.,284f.). An elective affinity exists between the social conditions of certain strata of society and the particular religious conceptions of those strata. So, the conception of Yahweh varied with different social groups ([1917–19]1952,133): the semi-nomad believed he accompanied the people wherever they went, the warrior saw him as a war god, the urban masses located him in the temple. Weber, however, never defined what he meant by elective affinity, and in fact the term seems paradoxical (see Thomas:1985,39–54): 'elective' implies the existence of free choice, but 'affinity' implies the mechanical or determined, non-elective, relationship between one thing and another. The interpretation of the term in this context has been the subject of some discussion. One understanding, which relates it directly to another aspect of Weber's sociology of religion, is that it refers to the process of 'routinization' by which an original charismatic innovation is integrated into culture: the 'elective' component is the free and undetermined idea of the charismatic; the 'affinity' component is the gradual adaptation of that idea to culture so that it becomes expressive of the interests of the group which holds it. Against this, however, it seems more likely that Weber understood routinization to imply a process of divergence in which the charismatic insight is elaborated and developed into a system which stands in increasing tension with culture (Thomas,*ibid.*; further below,46f.).

'Elective affinity' is in origin a chemical concept to do with the propensity of elements to combine with each other in certain ratios. Weber's use of it reflects its transference by Goethe, in his novel *Die Wahlverwandtschaften*, to the human sphere in order to describe the attraction of one person to another, their breaking apart and being drawn into new relationships. According to an interpretation of this novel, current in Weber's time, Goethe was concerned with themes such as chance and necessity, freedom and determinism, and by means of the concept he attempted to overcome the dualism inherent in these alternatives. Weber, according to Thomas, was probably well acquainted with this novel and that interpretation of it; his use of the idea may likewise reflect a desire to transcend a similar dualism of freedom and determinism in the question of the relationship of religion to social context. Through it Weber affirmed the inextricable interlocking of the socially determined and the individually free in the origin of religious ideas. It is, however, in the end simply a descriptive term rather than one useful in any analytic way.

In his biography of Weber, Bendix (1960,46f.) has quoted the German historian Otto Hintze as providing a formulation of Weber's perspective: all human action, whether political or religious, is rooted in material interests, but these cannot survive without the spiritual meaning and justification afforded by ideal interests. In similar vein, Weber himself argued (1948,280) that 'the "world images" that have been created by "ideas" have, like switchmen, determined the tracks along which action has been pushed by the dynamic of interest'. From such isolated observations, however, it is not possible to elaborate any clear theoretical presentation of Weber's view; but for the present, it is sufficient to indicate that an idealist interpretation is certainly not true to the complexity of his thought.

The structural-functionalist tradition

The sociology of Emile Durkheim

The differences between Durkheim and Weber may be summarized as follows: in Durkheim's understanding, social phenomena are realities to be explained only by other social phenomena, while for Weber they are to be explained by reference to the subjective intentions and actions of individuals (Lukes:1975,20 n.76). That social phenomena are for Durkheim *sui generis* realities implies that society is not to be understood by any form of biological or psychological reductionism; such a procedure operates on the unacceptable assumption that the non-social represents a deeper level of explanation than the social. An excellent example of what is meant by this is provided by Durkheim's study of suicide. He distinguished different forms of suicide, and related their incidence to a variety of social causes: egoistic suicide arises from a breakdown in cohesion and integration in the social community; anomic suicide arises from a breakdown of values or a condition of moral deregulation; altruistic suicide is related to honour and prestige. At no point was Durkheim interested primarily in the psychological state of the one who commits suicide; rather, he seeks its causes in what he calls the 'suicidal aptitude of each society'.

This approach has been taken to imply a thorough reification of society, granting it a concrete independent existence which it does not really have, and, indeed, although Durkheim often emphasized that society could not exist without the individuals who compose it, it is not a distortion of his thinking to say that in his view the sum which the aggregate of these individuals creates is something very different from a mere collection of parts. This theory of society is expressed already in Durkheim's early reviews of German social thinkers (see Giddens:1971,66ff.), and is explicit or implicit throughout his work: the language an individual uses, the currency he employs, the professional practices he follows, all exist independently of his own use of them (Durkheim:[1895]1964,2). The individual as such has no significant claim to priority. Society is the prior reality which determines the individual, materially, mentally and spiritually. Pre-social individual nature is characterized only by vague and general instincts; it is under the influence of society that these are given concrete and particular form (cf. Lukes:1975,122). It is only as social man that individual, physical man is knowable.

Durkheim developed his view within the framework of understanding two ideal types of society: one characterized by mechanical solidarity and the other by organic solidarity. The distinction between these types is a distinction in the degree of integration of the individual into society. Each individual, for Durkheim, has a double consciousness (*conscience*): one is the consciousness of the group as a whole, while the other is personal, individual consciousness. The stronger and more pervasive the collective consciousness, the weaker the individual consciousness (Durkheim:[1893]1933,129f.; cf. Lukes:1975,149). The collective consciousness comprises those beliefs and sentiments common to the members of a given society. In content it is pervasively religious (Durkheim, *ibid.*,169; cf. Lukes:1975,152). It is characteristic of societies in which the collective consciousness is strong that law should be of a penal or repressive form. Crime is an act which offends the collective consciousness, and punishment is a passionate reaction which has the function of maintaining social cohesion. In societies marked by such mechanical solidarity, law is the mechanism by means of which the collective consciousness acts upon individuals to maintain and strengthen their solidarity (Lukes:1975,160ff.; cf. also Rainer:1984).

The transition to a state of organic solidarity is brought about by a growth in differentiation among members of the society, which follows on an increase in density of the society. The density of society increases not simply through growth in numbers, but rather through the increasing concentration of the population in cities, and generally through the growth of community which brings the members of a society into ever closer contact. Thus, in so far as the transition from mechanical to organic solidarity implies historical change, it is by a process internal to society and is not the result of the volitional actions of individuals. Differentiation, together with the affective influence of the collective ideas of society back upon its members, brings about inevitable change. The concentration of individuals within a limited space leads to an increasingly intense struggle for survival; social differentiation is the peaceful means by which this struggle is resolved. Because each individual occupies his own place and plays his own role he is no longer in competition with others. The elimination of the weak and the survival of the strong, which is a necessary feature of the animal world, becomes unnecessary when individuals perform complementary rather than competitive functions in society (cf. Aron:1970,32; Lukes:1975,171). The descriptive term which Durkheim uses of such a society characterized by differentiation, namely 'organic solidarity', was already known in this context; it was a term which, in the light of Darwinian evolutionary theory, allowed a 'powerful combination of positivism and a perspective of evolutionary progress' (Giddens:1971,66).[2]

An index of the existence of organic solidarity in society is the decline of repressive law and the rise of restitutive law, that is, law which is concerned with the restoration of relationships to their normal state. This in turn presupposes that the collective consciousness of society is no longer so pervasive: crime is no longer a matter of offence against society as a whole, which society must punish in order to maintain its solidarity. This weakening of the collective consciousness, of the binding (religious) beliefs which had earlier characterized society, raises, however, the question of the nature of the unity implied in the description 'organic solidarity'. Durkheim was convinced that the analysis given by Tönnies of the nature of the unity of the *Gesellschaft*, that it was based on economic, contractual relationships, was inadequate as a definition of the unity of societies integrated by organic solidarity: a society based only on economic relationships would be chaotic; the proper functioning of economic contract presupposes norms and general moral commitments. Durkheim did not, however, reach a fully satisfactory alternative understanding of the nature of organic solidarity. In such societies the collective consciousness is more abstract and general (cf. Fenton:1984,32ff.), and has come to focus on the individual. It is now individualism as such which constitutes the bond of unity: each individual, freely and without social compulsion, performs the functions suited to his abilities. Such spontaneous division of labour, however, has not yet been generally achieved, and so, according to Durkheim, societies which have changed from a state of mechanical solidarity must be seen to be still in a process of transition to a future state of normal organic solidarity (Lukes:1975,163ff.,176f.; Giddens:1971,77ff.).

Religion and society in Durkheim's sociology
The major influence on Durkheim in the formulation of his views on religion was W. Robertson Smith.[3] The latter was thoroughly comparative and evolutionistic in his approach: he argued that societies go through a generally similar evolutionary process, and that earlier forms of advanced societies may be described by reference to primitive societies and also to the survivals from their own past which advanced societies exhibit. So, he understood totemism to be a phase of religious belief through which all societies pass. Sacrifice was the central and most basic rite in all religions, signifying an act of communion between a social group and its god. In the killing and eating of the totemic animal, which was the material representation of the clan, the clan celebrated and revitalized its unity.

This already hints at the broad outlines of Robertson Smith's understanding of the nature of religion and its relationship to society, which was to have a fundamental effect on Durkheim. The earliest social community was a religious community, and it confirmed and renewed its unity through ritual. Religion was a ritual system within the social order, comprising acts and

30

observances; it was not a body of dogma or formulated theology. The communion sacrifice was the central ritual, expressing and maintaining the unity of the cohesive, undifferentiated social group. Only when society later became stratified and differentiated, as a result of increased members and social density, were the gods alienated from men to become more like kings than kinsmen, and to be approached with sacrifices of gifts and tribute. Robertson Smith's single greatest contribution to social research has been described by Beidelman (1974) as his emphasis on the social basis of beliefs and values.

> A man did not choose his religion or frame it for himself; it came to him as part of the general scheme of social obligations and ordinances laid upon him, as a matter of course, by his position in the family and in the nation . . . A certain amount of religion was required of everybody; for the due performance of religious acts was a social obligation in which every one had his appointed share . . . Religion did not exist for the saving of souls but for the preservation and welfare of society . . . Every human being, without choice on his own part, but simply in virtue of his birth and upbringing, becomes a member of what we call a *natural* society. He belongs, that is, to a certain family and a certain nation, and this membership lays upon him definite obligations and duties which he is called upon to fulfil as a matter of course, and on pain of social penalties and disabilities, while at the same time it confers upon him certain rights and advantages. In this respect the ancient and modern worlds are alike; but there is this important difference, that the tribal or national societies of the ancient world were not strictly natural in the modern sense of the word, for the gods had their part and place in them equally with men. The circle into which a man was born was not simply a group of kinsfolk and fellow-citizens, but embraced also certain divine beings, the gods of the family and of the state, which to the ancient mind were as much a part of the particular community with which they stood connected as the human members of the social circle (Robertson Smith:1927,28f.).

Durkheim was directly indebted to Robertson Smith for major aspects of his understanding of the nature of religion and its relationship with society. The latter's theory of the totemic origin of sacrifice provided the framework within which Durkheim interpreted ethnographic evidence deriving from Australian aborigines, on the basis of which he could then argue that 'sacrifice was not founded to create a bond of artificial kinship between a man and his gods, but to maintain and renew the natural kinship which primitively united them' (Durkheim:[1912]1976,340). It is true that Durkheim went on to reject Robertson Smith's view that the sacrificial offering was a secondary development, presupposing a view of the gods as kings to whom tribute is due; rites of oblation 'are certainly among the most primitive that have ever been observed' (*ibid.*,341). Nevertheless, he firmly maintained the totemic and ritualistic understanding of primitive society and its unity which Robertson Smith had earlier expounded (cf. Lukes:1975,454f.).

For Durkheim, religious beliefs

> are always common to a determined group, which makes profession of adhering to them and of practising the rites connected with them. They are not merely received individually by all the members of this group; they are something belonging to the group, and they make its unity. The individuals who compose it feel themselves united to each other by the simple fact that they have a common faith (Durkheim, *ibid.*,43).

This is a definition of religion as a social fact and in terms of its social function; it clearly identifies religion with the content of the collective consciousness of society characterized by mechanical solidarity. Religion belongs to those collective representations of society into which individuals are born and which are imbued in the consciousness of those individuals: ideas of order, authority, morality, and even ideas of space and time are part of the collective consciousness existing independently of individuals (cf. Nisbet:1967,243ff.; Giddens:1971,105ff.,112ff.).

On this basis, Durkheim, therefore, arrived at the following formal definition of religion (*ibid.*,47): 'A religion is a unified system of beliefs and practices relative to sacred things, that is to say, things set apart and forbidden – beliefs and practices which unite into one single moral community called a Church, all those who adhere to them.' This definition may be taken to have three essential aspects. First, religion is concerned with the sacred rather than with the profane. Of this distinction between the sacred and the profane, which is the distinctive trait of all religious thought, Durkheim wrote (*ibid.*,38f.):

> *it is absolute*. In all the history of human thought there exists no other example of two categories of things so profoundly differentiated or so radically opposed to one another. The traditional opposition of good and bad is nothing beside this; for the good and the bad are only two opposed species of the same class, namely morals, just as sickness and health are two different aspects of the same order of facts, life, while the sacred and the profane have always and everywhere been conceived by the human mind as two distinct classes, as two worlds between which there is nothing in common.

Secondly, religion is not simply a system of beliefs and ideas as the rationalists understand it; it is also, and indeed primarily, a system of practices. The function of religion is not simply to make us think, to add to our knowledge, but rather to help us to live, to provide us with the strength 'to endure the trials of existence, or to conquer them'. Its primary character is not, therefore, the ideas, but rather its being that sphere within which we are brought into contact with the powers and influences of the sacred.

> Whoever has really practised a religion knows very well that it is the cult which gives rise to these impressions of joy, of interior peace, of serenity, of enthusiasm which are, for the believer, an experimental proof of his beliefs. The cult is not simply a system of signs by which the faith is outwardly translated; it is a collection of the means by which this is created and recreated periodically (Durkheim, *ibid.*,417).

Thirdly, religion functions to unite all its followers into a single moral community; it has a unitive and integrative function. This fundamental characteristic is that which distinguishes religion from magic. The latter also has beliefs and rites, and indeed it is often found diffused through large masses of the population. 'But it does not result in binding together those who adhere to

33

it, nor in uniting them into a group leading a common life' (Durkheim, *ibid.*,44). In so far as there are societies devoted to magic, they are societies of magicians, not societies embracing all the followers of magic, the clientele of the magician, into a single community. Those who consult the magician need have no relationship with one another, and even their contact with the magician is occasional; the moral community is an intrinsic characteristic of religion, not of magic.

Durkheim's high estimate of religion and its role in society clearly distinguishes him from positivists such as Comte; religion is no primitive science to be outgrown with advances in scientific understanding, but is essential to society and its continued functioning. This implies that in the matter of its origins also it should not be treated as simply primitive superstition. In the question of the source of religion, its original totemic nature is the significant point. Totemism is the most primitive type of religion known, and to discover its origins is to discover that which gives rise to the religious sentiment in humanity. Totemism recognizes three objects as sacred: the totem, which in itself may be an insignificant animal or plant; the representation of the totem which is displayed or carried; and the members of the clan which venerates the totem, for every member of the clan shares in the totem's sacredness and is believed to be genealogically related to the totem. Because the totem frequently has no intrinsic significance, its sacredness must stem from its symbolic nature, its being the material representation of something else. Since it is both a symbol of the god and a symbol of the whole clan group, it may be concluded that 'the god of the clan, the totemic principle, can therefore be nothing else than the clan itself, personified and represented to the imagination under the visible form of the animal or vegetable which serves as totem' (Durkheim, *ibid.*,206).

This is true of the origins of religion, and it holds good also for religion in its more advanced forms.

> In a general way, it is unquestionable that a society has all that is necessary to arouse the sensation of the divine in minds, merely by the power that it has over them; for to its members it is what a god is to his worshippers. In fact, a god is, first of all, a being whom men think of as superior to themselves, and upon whom they feel that they depend. Whether it be

a conscious personality, such as Zeus or Jahveh, or merely abstract forces such as those in play in totemism, the worshipper, in the one case as in the other, believes himself held to certain manners of acting which are imposed upon him by the nature of the sacred principle with which he feels that he is in communion. Now society also gives us the sensation of a perpetual dependence. Since it has a nature which is peculiar to itself and different from our individual nature, it pursues ends which are likewise special to it; but as it cannot attain them except through our intermediacy, it imperiously demands our aid. It requires that, forgetful of our own interests, we make ourselves its servitors, and it submits us to every sort of inconvenience, privation and sacrifice, without which social life would be impossible. It is because of this that at every instant we are obliged to submit ourselves to rules of conduct and of thought which we have neither made nor desired, and which are sometimes even contrary to our most fundamental inclinations and instincts (Durkheim, *ibid.*,206f.).

3

The Conflict Tradition in Old Testament Study

Max Weber

Introduction

Weber's *Ancient Judaism* was first published in a series of essays, at a late stage in his career, in 1917–19.[1] It has been judged to be a descriptive account of ancient Israel rather than a work of analytical or theoretical sociology (Rodd:1981,105 n.1), but to read it on that descriptive level only may involve the loss of some of the richness of sociological thinking on which it depends. It has a general approach and makes use of specific concepts which are nowhere clearly defined in the book, but which arise out of and presuppose Weber's earlier sociological studies. Weber himself notes (1952,425f.n.1) that the work makes no claim to present new facts; only some of the sociological perspectives applied to the facts are new. It is these sociological viewpoints, reflecting the preceding decades of Weber's sociological study, which deserve particular attention.

Weber studied Judaism as part of his analysis of the rise of capitalism. His much earlier work on *The Protestant Ethic and the Spirit of Capitalism*, which first appeared in 1904–05, had pointed to Calvinistic Protestantism as one factor involved. Ancient Israel, however, was argued to have anticipated Calvinistic Protestantism in two respects. First, Israel provided some of the essential ideas and conceptions which allowed for the rise of western civilization: its anti-magical attitude, transmitted to the West through the Hebrew Bible, provided the foundation for later rational and scientific development in the West (Petersen:1979,118f.). Secondly, the example of ancient Israel confirmed the complex relationship between religion and society characteristic of the relationship between Protestantism and capitalism: *The Protestant Ethic* was written in part to demonstrate the error of the (Marxist) materialist thesis that all ideas, including religious ideas, have a socio-economic materialist basis, and to show that the relationship between ideas and social conditions, between religion and society, is in fact much more complex; *Ancient Judaism* confirmed this view.

Weber's form of historical sociology involved first the definition of a situation and then the tracing of its origins. In *Ancient Judaism* he first defined the nature of the post-exilic Jewish community and then sought its origins in the history of ancient Israel. The Jewish community is described by two key terms: status group and pariah community. It is not an economic class, nor a political party, but a status group. By this is meant a group which has no necessary economic unity but is held together by a common life style expressing itself in particular ways: positively, in certain common beliefs and customary practices, and, negatively, in restrictions in the spheres of marriage and dietary habits. A pariah community is a status group, and Weber proposed that this is the most appropriate classification for the Jewish community. This description is used with caution, however, for by contrast with the Hindu caste system, in which context the term 'pariah people' is normally used, the Jewish community was governed by a rational religious ethic free from all magical ideas; moreover, the Jews were a pariah people in a caste free world, and had willingly adopted their status as a pariah people (1952,3f.).[2]

Weber's ideal type approach to Israelite origins
In his quest for the origins of this Jewish community, Weber returns to the formative period of ancient Israel in Palestine. His discussion presupposes an awareness of his particular sociological method, a method which here remains unexpressed. Following a description of the social structure of nomadic bedouin, cities in Palestine, the peasant farmer and the semi-nomadic herdsman, he turns to the laws of the Book of the Covenant and Deuteronomy and then to the subject of the covenant. The relationship between these topics, and in particular

the question of how they impinge on Israel, is far from clear. The life of nomadic bedouin is understood to be irrelevant to ancient Israel, but the discussion of the social structure of the cities, the peasant farmer and the semi-nomadic herdsman, which are portrayed as ways of life hostile to one another, relates them to Israelites and to non-Israelites apparently quite indiscriminately. Where Israel is actually to be found within these mutually antagonistic social contexts remains obscure.

Weber approaches history here, following his usual method, from the perspective of the ideal type. This, he argues, is no new procedure, but rather one which makes explicit what the historian has always automatically and unconsciously done in practice; by making it explicit, however, the historian can be more precise and unambiguous in the concepts, models or ideal types which he uses (1949,92f.). Weber's ideal type is, as already noted, a theoretical construction with a heuristic function:

> An ideal type is constructed by the abstraction and combination of an indefinite number of elements which, although found in reality, are rarely or never discovered in this specific form . . . Such an ideal type is neither a 'description' of any definite aspect of reality, nor, according to Weber, is it a hypothesis; but it can aid in both description and explanation. An ideal type is not, of course, ideal in a normative sense: it does not convey the connotation that its realisation is desirable . . . An ideal type is a pure type in a logical and not an exemplary sense . . . The creation of ideal types is in no sense an end in itself; . . . the only purpose of constructing it is to facilitate the analysis of empirical questions (Giddens: 1971,141f.; cf.Schäfer-Lichtenberger:1983,24ff.).

So, within the framework of his ideal type approach to social structures in Palestine, Weber is not in the first instance describing Israelite cities, Israelite farmers or Israelite semi-nomads; rather, he is creating social types. The question of their possible national, ethnic or religious identity is secondary.

Weber distinguished four types of society which could be set on a spectrum. At one end is the type of the desert bedouin. This type, however, has little relevance for Israel; it comprises desert dwellers who have always scorned agriculture and settlement, and have no state organization. At the other end of the spectrum there is the city. Its structure may be described on the basis of the Amarna texts, Old Testament records on both pre-monarchic and monarchic periods, and information on the Mediterranean city-states from classical sources. In its fully developed form the city was a fortress. Basic to its social structure was the clan, as in bedouin society; but in the city there was not the same equality of life. Powerful clans gained the ascendancy, with the head of the most powerful clan holding the position of *nasi* or prince. He ruled the city, sharing power with the elders of the other clans and the family heads of his own clan. From such politically powerful clans derived the *gibborim* or *bene hayil*, a group which Weber calls the urban patriciate. The urban patriciate in the city also held sway over the countryside around the city, living off the rents from their lands and acquiring wealth through control of the trade routes. This led to the creation of a class distinction between the urban patrician as creditor and the rural peasant as debtor.

This example illustrates both how ideal types are constructed and also the potential weaknesses in the approach. In Weber's presentation the city type is an independent form in which society is divided between patricians and plebeians. While significant information is derived from the Old Testament, these two essential characteristics, the independence of the city and its social divisions, are in fact taken from classical history. The justification for the procedure is that whatever the particular nature of any given situation might be, these represent the essential traits of the type, and so establish the perspective from which any given example must be seen. For the historian of ancient Israel it may well be that all the characteristics described by Weber cannot be accepted as effectively present in Israel's cities; but these characteristics, nevertheless, point to the tendency and internal dynamics of the structure to which Israel's cities, like those of Greece and Rome, belonged.[3]

By contrast with the city, the other two social types are constructed on the basis of Old Testament materials only. The type of the peasantry is attested especially in the Song of Deborah. It had some political and military organization, but otherwise we know nothing of the political and economic conditions of the free peasants nor anything of any possible social differentiation within the type. The peasantry had once formed the kernel of the army of the Israelite confederacy, but with increasing urbanization and the changeover to chariot warfare techniques, it seems that the political and military significance of the peasantry declined. Their economic exploitation by the urban patricians and exclusion from those political rights which depended on property ownership, meant that they were reduced to the class of plebeians and debt slaves.

Finally, there is the type of the semi-nomadic stock breeder. Its social structure resembled that of the bedouin: a number of families constituted a clan which functioned to guarantee personal safety; the tribe was a coalescence of clans which came together temporarily under a charismatic leader in time of threat or in order to extend grazing grounds. Their relationship with the settled population is described by the term *ger*. This social group included all landless people (Levites, potters, carpenters, weavers, and those who later emerge as guilds of singers), but especially small stock-breeding herdsmen; they were aliens who lived under certain rights of protection. Their relationship with the settled community was regulated by treaty, which covered particularly grazing rights and rights of migration through the agricultural areas. Such relationships could readily lead to full citizenship and urbanization of the wealthier clans. Again, as in the case of the peasantry, so the significance of the semi-nomadic form of life declined. Political developments and the curtailment of pasture land led to the decline of semi-nomadism and the demilitarization of the herdsmen who, along with the rural peasantry, came to form the poor plebeians or proletariat. This economic and social decline of the semi-nomads finds its reflection in the presentation of the patriarchs as powerless and peaceful *gerim* who lived as small stock-breeders among military burghers.

No one of these types is identified historically by Weber as Israel; it is within the context of all of them that the historical Israel is to be empirically located. Once one begins to speak of Israel one moves away from the typological approach, which by nature is static and timeless, to the historical approach, which by nature presupposes movement and development. Israel was a historical entity, a shifting and heterogeneous population which, within the framework of a developing urbanism, is variously represented within all these types. Developing Israelite urbanism is reflected especially in the pre-exilic collections of law (1952,61). This reference to the Old Testament collections of law is of crucial importance for the historical identification of Israel within the social types described. The primary concern of the Book of the Covenant is with peasant property in cattle and with the protection of one peasant's property from damage by the animals of another. The laws also regulate, however, money loans and deposits, the taking of interest, and so they have in view not just the peasant in isolation. Rather, the laws focus on the peasant in his relations with other social groups, especially the urban patriciate which would have been the source of such loans. Similarly, the laws regulate the peasant's obligations towards the *ger*, including semi-nomadic herdsmen. The very existence of the Book of the Covenant reflects the need for codification arising from social tension and antagonism between different social groups within the developing society of Israel(1952,65), whose ongoing social evolution is clearly reflected in the revision of the Book of the Covenant in Deuteronomy.

Thus, while the primary concern of the Book of the Covenant is with the situation of the peasant on his own land, this does not mean that Israel is simply a peasant agricultural society; the law has in view also the developing urban patriciate on the one hand and the *ger* on the other. Israel is to be found in the city, in the peasantry, and among semi-nomadic herdsmen, and it is in order to regulate relations between these distinct social types within Israel that the Book of the Covenant exists. Nor can Israel be said to have been first semi-nomadic, then peasant, and then urban; rather, all types existed at the same time within Israel, a people which in general terms was in the process of a gradual development towards urbanization (1952,42).

These, however, were mutually antagonistic social forms: hostility existed both between the cities of the plains and the peasants in the mountain areas, and between the agricultural peasants and the semi-nomadic small stock-breeders. The Song of Deborah reflects these hostilities: the stock-breeding, non-agricultural east Jordanian tribes of Reuben and Gilead had no interest in the battle; nor did the coastal dwelling, and early urbanized tribe of Asher and the urban tribe of Dan. It is the agricultural peasants who bear the burden of the battle with the cities. The question must then arise: what is it that allowed for the existence of an Israel which could overcome such antagonisms and comprehend such social diversity? Weber found the clue to the answer in the law codes of the Old Testament, and especially in the increasingly theological elaboration which these laws exhibit. As the laws gradually develop to meet changing situations they become more explicitly laws of Yahweh. They are not simply laws regulating social relations; they are laws of the covenant between Yahweh and Israel. It is on this that Israel's original unity is founded, on a union of different groups in covenant with Yahweh.

In order to account for the emergence of this covenant unity, Weber comes to an obscure conclusion (1952,79f.): it is not the life conditions of the original Israelites which gave rise to the covenant, which could then be seen as the ideological expression of those conditions; rather, once the covenant was established, those life conditions afforded it the best opportunity of survival; the actual origins of the covenant go back to religious-historical situations which may often have been personal. Apparently, Weber means by this, first, that by a relationship, which could be described as 'elective affinity', the Yahweh covenant won acceptance and was maintained by social strata whose social and economic form of life was such as to ensure its survival; and, secondly, that the origin of the covenant conception lies in personal experiences of a religious and historical nature. By the latter he seems to mean the exodus from Egypt and the role of Moses, as charismatic prophet and leader, in that event (1952,118).

On this crucial point, the first stage in the emergence of Israel as a pariah people, when a covenant was established by Moses to bind a human group of diverse social components to Yahweh as its God, Weber seems in the end inconclusive and ambiguous. In the light of his general sociological approach, however, it is possible to supplement his description of the emergence of Israel with two further points. First, the understanding of the individuals who constituted that emergent Israel are of foundational importance, and it is to that understanding that sociology must in the end come. It is the understandings and interpretations held by individuals of their experiences and circumstances which constitute the creative and dynamic forces behind the first appearance of the new society of Israel. Secondly, what we have in the Book of the Covenant and Deuteronomy represent progressive rationalizations of the original charismatic foundation. The charismatic founder may no longer be directly accessible to us, but his presence is presupposed and required by these rationalizations. The achievement of the charismatic, Moses, was a breakthrough shaped by personal interests and experiences, to a basic insight from which new social and historical situations could be confronted, a breakthrough which came to be realized historically in the creation of what Weber described, adopting a term from Wellhausen (see Schäfer-Lichtenberger:1983,128), as the *Eidgenossenschaft*, the oath or covenant community of Israel.

Prophecy and the establishment of the pariah community
In Weber's understanding, Yahweh was not a local or tribal deity familiar from of old, but was always a god from afar (see Fahey:1982,64f.). Originally conceived of as a war god (corresponding to the purposes of the confederacy), full of demonic, superhuman power, his image was sublimated and rationalized as a result of two influences in particular. First, ideas of supreme heavenly deities, to be found in Israel's immediate environment, were carried over to Yahweh. More significantly, however, there took place a rationalization of the nature and will of Yahweh, particularly through the work of the Levites.[4] In their pastoral role they responded to the needs of the community, making known the means by which misfortunes might be averted, and so the proper ritual of the worship of Yahweh and the rational knowledge of his commandments were disseminated through Israel. Israel's worship of Yahweh was characterized primarily by obedience to his commandments proclaimed by the Levites; sacrifice, in Weber's view (1952,427; cf. Fahey:1982,66f.), did not have fundamental significance for ancient Israel.

The technical means available to the Levites for discerning the will of Yahweh, the casting of lots yielding a yes or no answer to specific questions, had the effect of promoting rational questions concerning specific issues and of minimizing emotional and mystic irrationalism. Thus, there accumulated both the rational knowledge of the will of Yahweh in the form of divine commandments and the ritualistic means to amend offences against them. It is this levitical teaching of the laws and commandments of the covenant between Yahweh and Israel, culminating in the ethical decalogue and the development of a rational 'workaday ethic of the masses' (Weber:1952,249), which formed the source of the ethic of the classical prophets. They preached the levitic ethic, the general knowledge of which they all assumed (*ibid.*, 278).

The prophet is defined by Weber as 'a purely individual bearer of charisma, who by virtue of his mission proclaims a religious doctrine or divine commandment' (1965,46). He is distinguished from other religious functionaries by a variety of features, including the unremunerated nature of his activity, but especially by his having received a personal call. As there is a distinction between mystical and ascetic religious systems, however, so there is a distinction between two types of prophet: the one is represented by the Buddha, the other by Muhammed. In the former case he is an 'exemplary man who, by his personal example, demonstrates to others the way to religious salvation . . . The preaching of this type of prophet says nothing about a divine mission or an ethical duty of obedience, but rather directs itself to the self-interest of those who crave salvation, recommending to them the same path as he himself traversed.' In the case of Muhammed, he is an ethical prophet, 'an instrument for the proclamation of a god and his will', demanding obedience as an ethical duty (1965,55).

The Israelite prophet is an ethical prophet. There is never present here any sense of mystical possession by or communion with God; rather, God is experienced only as command. Nor is there any sense of removal from the world; rather, the Israelite prophet is the devoted servant of the divine command in the world (Weber:1952,312ff.).

In the context of Weber's understanding of religion there is a particular problem with his description of Israelite prophecy. He contends that in Israelite prophecy there is never any questioning of the meaning of the world or of life, nor any idea of a mystical interpretation of existence. For Weber, however, religion is in general concerned with questions of meaning, and it is the conflict between religious meaning and empirical reality which produces prophecy; prophecy marks a breakthrough to a new level of meaning. In the case of Israel, the conflict was between the meaning of the world proposed by Israelite religion and the empirical threat to her existence posed by Assyria and Babylon, and without this conflict the prophets would never have emerged. This can mean only that the threat to her life created for Israel an overwhelming problem of meaning, with which existing religious beliefs could not cope, and which the prophets came forward to answer. If the threat had constituted solely a problem of survival, the response would have been the building up of armies and defence works; that it constituted also a problem of meaning is clear from the nature of the prophetic response, for this response dealt not with Israel's defence but with her proper conduct before a punishing God. Meaning thus does seem to be, even in Weber's thinking, the motivating force behind the emergence of classical prophecy.[5]

The resolution of the inconsistency is not certain; it is probable that Weber intended to emphasize how, in contrast with the mystical gnosis and esoteric knowledge of exemplary prophecy, for which 'meaning' consisted in rejection of the world and mystical union with the divine, the ethical prophets of Israel offered no such route to salvation but rather directed their hearers solely to the divine commandments. Absolute obedience to the divine demand in the world, a demand which was known to both prophets and hearers from levitical preaching and teaching, a demand to be obeyed simply because it came from God, was the only way to salvation. This ethical demand of the prophets, however, emerges from, and is considered by Weber to reflect, an understanding of order in creation with which the reality of Israel's life does not conform; the problem with which prophecy deals is 'the conflict between empirical reality and this conception of the world as a meaningful totality', and prophetic revelation 'involves for both the prophet himself and for his followers . . . a unified view of the world derived from a consciously integrated and meaningful attitude toward life' (Weber:1965,58f.).

There are two further issues relating to prophecy which arise out of the foregoing, and on these Weber made a contribution with particularly sociological significance. The first concerns the social setting from which the prophets derived, and the second the reception of the prophetic message into their social contexts. It is in relation to the second of these that the direct relevance of prophecy to the emergence of the pariah people, in Weber's understanding, emerges.

Weber rejected any identification of the prophets with particular political or social groups. Even though the political situation in Israel gave the essential context for their religious message, it is out of the question for Weber that the prophets should be placed in or identified with proletarian or negatively privileged or uneducated strata (1952,277f.). Weber justified this both by appeal to the direct evidence of the Old Testament, which often suggests a high social standing for some of the prophets, and also on general sociological grounds. It has already been noted (above,25) that for Weber neither the peasantry nor the nobility can be understood as the originators of new religious conceptions or as the carriers of rational, ethical movements. The lot of the peasant is bound up with nature; the religious interest of the nobility is restricted to its function in legitimizing their privileged social situation. Rather, it is the economic life of the middle class, the artisan and the merchant, which inclines them in the direction of a rational, ethical religion. This does not mean that for Weber the prophets were essentially of that social stratum; rather, it is that social stratum which served as the carrier of the prophetic ethic. As far as the emergence of that ethic is concerned, Weber argued only in general terms that the essential conditions for new religious ideas are that men still have the capacity to question the meaning of events, and that this is possible only away from the centres of the great powers and cultures (1952,206f.). It was in a situation of marginality over against the great culture centre of Egypt that the roots of what was to become Judaism emerged; it was in a similar situation of marginality over against the great culture centres of Assyria and Babylon that the new religious conceptions at the heart of Israelite prophecy made their appearance. It was particularly in the marginalized context of Israel that the charismatic innovation of ethical prophecy could take place.

The second issue on which Weber had a distinctive sociological view related to the reception of the prophetic message into a social context. The prophetic proclamation marks a breakthrough, or a sudden leap forward; it is followed by a period in which the proclamation is absorbed and systematized in the religious following which succeeded the prophet. Weber referred to this as the 'routinization' of prophecy (1965,60ff.). This is the process by which 'the doctrine of the prophets enters into everyday life, as the function

46

of a permanent institution' (*ibid.*,62); it denotes the process which results in the prophetic insight becoming established as the right understanding.

This should not be taken to imply the integration of religion into society and culture, the religious ethical demand of the prophet gradually becoming adapted to the social and economic realities of the day. Rather, in Weber's view (1948,323ff.), tension between religion and the world tends to increase rather than decrease. The process of routinization of prophecy represents the transformation of a revealed religion into a priestly enterprise characterized by pastoral care and the religious cultivation of the individual. So, while it is true that for Weber the charismatic is one who achieves a breakthrough, this should not be understood to mean that he held a theory of culture and history according to which such breaks were then followed by periods of stability when the new insight was routinized into society in the form of institutions. Rather, the charismatic breakthrough and its routinization relate to the mode by which the religious implications of the prophetic proclamation for everyday life are developed by religious leaders. It is at the charismatic point of inception that religion and culture are most closely integrated, in that it is then that historical and social experience is given the 'right' meaning which can become established; in the routinization of the prophetic proclamation into specific prescriptions of a casuistical kind there emerges a tension between religious meaning and empirical experience, which in time forms the eventual context of emergence of a new prophetic (charismatic) proclamation.

The routinization of prophecy, as a function of the priesthood, represents that process and that relationship in which Moses stands with the levitical preachers and teachers who succeeded him; it represents also that process and that relationship in which the priesthood and the post-exilic Jewish community stand with pre-exilic prophecy. The teaching of the prophets, especially their insistence that Israel's destruction was the will of Yahweh who was using the world powers, made clearly explicit the latent monotheism and universality of the Israelite idea of God; this teaching also expressed the idea of humility and absolute obedience as the only mode of relationship with God. The renunciation of self-help, and passive trust in Yahweh alone, are distinctive characteristics of the post-exilic pariah community which may thus be seen to be directly rooted in pre-exilic prophecy.

The lines of communication in Weber's thinking are far from clear here (see Schmueli:1969,176ff.; Petersen:1979,129ff.), but in this respect a definite link between pre-exilic prophecy and post-exilic Judaism can be established: the pre-exilic prophets had been vindicated in the events of 587 BC, and so the exilic and post-exilic prophets commanded respect. The pre-exilic proclamation of reliance on Yahweh alone together with the preaching of Second Isaiah that the ignominious fate of Israel was the means for the realization of Yahweh's plan encouraged humility and self-abasement, and put a high evaluation on blameless suffering. All of these Weber saw as decisive contributions to the pariah status of post-exilic Judaism.[6] The life style of this community was also marked, however, by a voluntary segregation from the surrounding society; this was expressed and maintained through the prohibition of mixed marriage and through dietary regulations, as well as through an economic ethos which distinguished between those within and those outside the community (Deut.23:19f.[Heb.20f.]). While much of this reflected traditional ritualism in Israel, there was this significant difference: the distinction between the *ger* and the full citizen is broken down, and the *ger* has become a full member of the post-exilic Jewish community. This abolition of the separate status of the *ger* took place in the context of Israel's transformation from a political community into a religious community, in which all Israel came to take on the status of the *ger* over against the larger society in which it now existed as a pariah people. This development was one brought about not just by external political and military events, but by an internal transformation whose major roots are to be led back to pre-exilic prophecy.

The conflict tradition in later Old Testament study

Introduction

For a number of reasons, Weber's work did not have the immediate widespread impact which might have been expected. Biblical study, under the influence of Barth, was beginning to become more concerned with biblical theology rather than with biblical sociology and history; moreover, *Ancient Judaism* is itself at the very least 'dense and contorted' (Frick and Gottwald:1983,152), and this can scarcely have helped the popularization of the approach which it represented. The book was strongly attacked by Caspari (1922), who considered that it vastly overemphasized the role of the military covenant of the tribes in the origins of Yahwism, and underemphasized the creative and innovative element in the prophetic proclamation of the possible end of the relationship between Yahweh and Israel. It was, however, generally sympathetically reviewed by Guttmann even though he too had some substantial points of criticism to make. These related especially to: the political significance which Weber ascribed to the covenant (Israel already existed, Guttmann believed, before the covenant with Yahweh); the treatment of the Israelite cities from the perspective of the Greek *polis*; the failure to admit the existence of an idea of God in Israel before he was thought of as covenant God; the role assigned to the Levites in the development of the rational ethic proclaimed by the prophets; the characterization of the prophetic demand for humility, trust in God and renunciation of self-help as plebeian (Guttmann:1925,195ff.).

Guttmann's criticisms touched on some of the most characteristic and significant aspects of Weber's work, and, from the vantage point of the present, it can readily be appreciated how *Ancient Judaism* in fact represented a considerable break with the contemporary scholarly approaches which Guttmann more accurately reflected. In particular, the evolutionary approach of Wellhausen, for whom covenant represented a deuteronomic theologoumenon to be set within a developing legalism in Israel's religion, which represented a sharp contrast with the freedom and spontaneity of earlier belief and practice, was effectively rejected by Weber. Religious covenant is the foundation of Israel's social and political existence rather than a gradually emerging theological idea. This is a break with evolutionism which was to have, in time, a considerable influence on scholarly understanding of Israel's history and religion.

Israelite society in the conflict tradition
1. Weber's work proved extraordinarily productive and influential in the writings of two Old Testament scholars, Alt and his pupil Noth. Their work can scarcely be called consciously sociological, in the sense in which that term is here being used,

and so will not be reviewed as fully as, within other contexts, it wholly deserves. Nevertheless, it is certainly worth referring to at this point in order to indicate how Weber's particular perspectives could be useful in historical reconstruction and in fact became established in Old Testament scholarship. Three topics must be mentioned: the charismatic, the ideal type city-state, and Israel as an oath or covenant community. The first two appear especially in the work of Alt, and the third in that of Noth.

Alt understood charisma as the personal endowment or property of an individual, and used the term with reference both to the deliverers of Israel in the pre-monarchic period (Alt:[1930]1966,178; cf. Noth:1950,404ff.; 1960,101; Mayes: 1974,77,85), and to forms of kingship in the later northern kingdom of Israel (Alt:[1930]1966,189ff.; [1951]1966,243ff.). The term was taken to imply that the nature of leadership in both pre-monarchic and monarchic contexts was wholly personal and individual; it was quite distinct from the traditional leadership of the tribal elders, on the one hand, and from the dynastic-bureaucratic style which kingship adopted in the southern kingdom, on the other. The deliverers Ehud, Gideon, Jephthah, Samson, were individual charismatic leaders who came forward to meet specific emergencies and, having successfully completed their task, retired into their former obscurity. They occupied no institutional office and surrounded themselves with no administrative machinery; their authority was vested in themselves alone. Saul, often described as the last of the deliverers and first of the kings, was in fact a leader of this type. He differed from his predecessors only in that he was given permanent leadership to meet an enduring crisis, but, as with his predecessors, his authority was personal and individual, depending upon divine designation and popular acclamation. His was charismatic kingship, quite distinct from the dynastic form of monarchy founded by David. Saul's son, Ishbosheth, was not generally recognized as king and was set up only by the strength of Abner the army commander; once that support was removed, however, his illegitimate kingship was doomed.

Saul's kingship was understood by Alt to represent a style of kingship which was restored, though only in the northern kingdom, after the death of Solomon: it was based on personal charisma and thus required both divine designation and the acknowledgement of the people. So Jeroboam was anointed by Ahijah and acclaimed by the northern tribes as king (1 Kings 11f.). His son Nadab, however, enjoyed neither divine designation nor popular acclamation, and, although reported as having reigned for two years (1 Kings 15:25), was not truly king but only the interim occupant of the throne until the rise of a new charismatic leader, Baasha. The pattern was repeated, for after Baasha's twenty-four year reign his son Elah occupied the throne for only two years before his assassination by Zimri. The latter, however, reigned for only seven days before he was replaced by Omri. At this stage the pattern of charismatic kingship was broken: Omri's son succeeded him, and was followed by his sons Ahaziah and Jehoram, the dynasty being brought to an end eventually by the revolt of Jehu. This change in style of kingship was, according to Alt, closely associated with a particular feature of Omri's kingship, his establishment of a new capital city; this precisely paralleled the earlier capture of Jerusalem by David, and David also was the founder of a dynasty. It is at this point that the second topic on which Alt came under Weber's influence becomes particularly relevant.

Although Weber acknowledged that the city could be a small fortified agricultural community with a market, little different from a village, and presumably thus very much integrated into the surrounding countryside, he went on to describe the type of the city very much in terms of the Mediterranean *polis*. So the city was not only a fortress, the seat of the army, the local deity and priesthood, the monarchic and military authorities, but above all it was an independent social structure. The chief fortified city had a number of dependent rural towns; the urban patricians controlled the countryside both politically and economically, living off the rents of their lands which were cultivated for them by slaves or part tenants. This understanding of the Israelite city was largely taken over by Alt, at least for the monarchic period and especially with regard to Jerusalem and Samaria (Alt [1930]1966,217ff.; [1951]1966,248ff.; cf. Schäfer-Lichtenberger:1983,369ff.). When David captured Jerusalem from the Jebusites, and made it the capital of his empire, he did so not with the armies of the tribes but with his own men who owed loyalty to him alone. Thus, the city became legally the property of David alone, the city of David, and was never incorporated into the tribal territories. It remained an independent city-state within Israel, and, as the private property of David by right of conquest, it was legally his city and the city of his descendants after him. It was thus that David's kingship was necessarily, in Jerusalem first and then in Judah which accepted that situation, a dynastic kingship.

A closely similar situation emerged in the northern kingdom in the time of Omri (1 Kings 16:24). Omri 'bought the hill of Samaria from Shemer for two talents of silver; and he fortified the hill, and called the name of the city which he built, Samaria, after the name of Shemer, the owner of the hill'. Samaria was Omri's private property by right of purchase and similarly belonged to his descendants after him. It too formed an independent unit within Israel, and on this basis dynastic kingship was also established in the northern kingdom. It was a situation recognized even by Jehu, who brought the dynasty of Omri to an end, for, rather than conquer Samaria by force, he negotiated with its ruling families, as with an independent state, to hand over to him the surviving sons of Ahab (2 Kings 10).

Noth's indebtedness to Weber was particularly significant in relation to what became a widely accepted understanding of the nature of Israel in the pre-monarchic period. The suggestion that Israel in the pre-monarchic period had an amphictyonic structure was already familiar in Old Testament scholarship before Noth's work; Noth gave the theory a detailed and persuasive presentation (Noth:1930; 1960,85ff.; cf. Mayes:1974), and this he did largely under the influence of Weber's sociological perspective. The immediately obvious point of contact is that just as Weber saw pre-monarchic Israel as an oath community, deliberately created out of a variety of socio-economic types, so Noth presented amphictyonic Israel as a covenant community deliberately established out of formerly independent clans and tribes. In both cases, Israel is presented as a new religious community constituted by its covenant relationship with Yahweh. The 'amphictyony' is a classical structure applied by analogy, but it is an analogy which is applied with the help of Weberian categories. Both Weber and Noth (1930,40f.) think in terms of existing 'raw material' which is used in order to create new institutions; both are similarly vague about how and by whom that raw material is used; in both what is implied is the irruption into history of new institutions founded by charismatic individuals.

In two further respects Noth also reflects Weber's understanding. First, although the amphictyony analogy allowed Noth to elaborate on the nature of pre-monarchic Israel and its religious and political institutions in a much more detailed way than was possible for Weber, it is highly significant that for Noth as for Weber the account of Israel begins with Israel in the land. Weber begins with a discussion of types of society in the land; Noth begins with the constitution of the tribes in the land; for both, Israel's history begins with Israel in the land. Noth then systematically developed his view (1948; 1960,110ff.) in order to show how within the context of amphictyonic Israel in the land the traditions of pre-settlement time were given a national frame of reference and a chronological ordering as the definitive account of Israel's origins. This was an exercise carried out from the perspective established by Weber, for whom also the older material represented the old traditions of an Israel which came into existence only in the land.

Secondly, just as Noth saw amphictyonic Israel as the real and true Israel, which survived through the monarchic period, to which the monarchy represented a foreign institution, which was the focus of the traditions and laws of the Pentateuch, and to which the office of 'Judge of Israel' must be related, so also Weber had already argued (1952,205ff.) that the development of Yahwism took place in the interaction of an intellectual class with a demilitarized and socially declassed public which had suffered under the monarchy, a public which had formerly been the free confederates of the Israelite oath community. It was within this context, according to Weber, that the JE traditions and Deuteronomy belonged; Yahweh remained the God of the confederates and not of the dynasty (Weber:1952,194ff.). For both Weber and Noth the monarchy was an institution alien to the descendants of the pre-monarchic confederacy.

2. The work of Alt and Noth has dominated the study of ancient Israel until the present. It has not, however, generally been noted that it is a particular historical and sociological perspective, that of Weber, and not simply a range of historical data, which has through their work become established in Old Testament study. The historical studies of Alt and Noth represent a way of understanding Israelite history, and, however persuasive it may be, it must be evaluated as a methodology alongside other

possible methodologies. Even within the context of its own method, however, that of the conflict tradition represented especially by Weber, it has come under considerable scrutiny, which has resulted in certain refinements and even fundamental revisions. It is to these that some reference will now be made, following the order of sociological topics already noted as characteristic of their work.

In recent Old Testament study the term charisma has come to be used almost exclusively of the form of pre-monarchic tribal leadership together with the monarchic rule of Saul and some of the later kings of the northern kingdom. Weber provided a general sociological treatment of the phenomenon of charisma as one type of leadership or authority, but it was of the prophets rather than of the pre-monarchic deliverers that he chiefly used the term in relation to ancient Israel. Its use for the type of the pre-monarchic leader is now widespread; it has received particular attention from Weisman (1977) and Malamat (1976).

Weisman's study in many respects reflects the tendency to use the phrase 'charismatic leadership' as the description of an empirical historical situation: it was a form of leadership which emerged to meet situations of crisis with which the traditional leadership of the elders could not cope. Traditional and charismatic leadership represent two different systems in tension with each other. A balance between them was achieved by the introduction of a new office, that of the minor judge. This judicial and executive office was influenced by the tribal elders, in that most of the judges were elders of clans, and to it some of the charismatic leaders were also appointed. Thus, a new and more centralized system of leadership was created.

Similarly, Malamat has emphasized that charismatic activity belongs to times of psychic, physical, economic, ethical, religious or political distress or crisis, while part of its background is also to be found in the weakening of traditional authority within clans and tribes as a result of adaptation to the new conditions of settlement in Canaan. The particular importance of Malamat's study, however, lies in his discussion of charisma from a sociological perspective. In the first place, he follows Weber in emphasizing that the description of charismatic authority as exclusive, personal, independent of hierarchic structure, sporadic, unstable and transient, is the description of an ideal type. The charismatic type does not appear historically in pure form, but overlaps with other types: legal-rational and traditional forms of authority also contain charismatic traits. Thus, the historical question relates to the degree of charismatic quality, whether intense or attenuated, which is present in the different empirical forms that leadership may take. Secondly, Malamat has also noted that charismatic leadership is not to be explained simply by reference to times of distress. Also essential is the potential leader, someone who is able 'to satisfy the "charismatic hunger" of his contemporaries' (1976,156), by defining for them their hopes and aspirations (*ibid.*, 159f.). Malamat is thus able to construct a paradigm, within which the type of charismatic leadership belongs. It includes: a situation of crisis, a leader who can identify with the symbols held most sacred by the people, occasional public signs confirming the authority of the charismatic, spontaneous personal authority, independence from social structures and important religious and social centres, voluntary submission of the people.

This is a significant treatment of the subject, which, through restoring the sociological understanding of charisma as an ideal type, makes possible its continued fruitful application. Alt's discussion, and particularly his use of the category to distinguish the nature of monarchy in northern Israel from that in Judah, isolated charisma as an empirical, historical form which could be contrasted with dynastic kingship. This, however, could be shown to be unjustified on empirical grounds (Thornton:1963,1ff.; Buccellati:1967,195ff.), which in turn could be taken to imply the unsuitability of the term charisma for this context. Saul's monarchy was dynastic; he was succeeded by his son Ishbaal who was truly king, and recognized as such by Israelites. If he differed from Saul it was simply because Saul was the founder of a dynasty, whereas Ishbaal was not; but his right to kingship was not questioned by those who wished to assert a charismatic as opposed to a dynastic principle. Similarly, kingship in northern Israel was always understood as dynastic kingship. There were frequent changes of ruler, but these were the result of conspiracies leading to the overthrow of the preceding 'house' or dynasty (1 Kings 15:29;16:21f.); they were not the rejection of non-charismatic rulers and the rise of new charismatic kings.

Kingship was by nature dynastic kingship, but this does not mean that it was then non-charismatic. Empirical, historical forms may incorporate the traits of a number of types which, on a theoretical level, may be described as distinct. By maintaining the distinction between the empirical and the theoretical levels it is, therefore, possible to preserve the term and to use it not only of pre-monarchic forms of leadership, but also of monarchic rule whether in Israel or in Judah (cf. also Overholt:1984,287ff.). The description of a historical instance of rule or leadership as charismatic is a formal classification of that instance on the grounds that there is sufficient reason to believe that its essential nature is charismatic; such a judgment cannot be taken to exclude the possibility of the presence also of traditional and legal-rational elements in that same instance of rule. As far as pre-monarchic leadership is concerned, the classification of Ehud as a charismatic is not incompatible with the probability that already before his charismatic deliverance of Israel he was a recognized (traditional?) leader, and for that reason was the one who brought tribute to Eglon (Judg.3:17); as far as the monarchy is concerned, charismatic kingship does not imply that the king in question must have come to the throne by means other than dynastic succession; charisma and dynastic succession are not then to be taken as incompatible forms of leadership.

3. Alt's application of the ideal type city-state to Jerusalem and Samaria has been examined by Buccellati (1967, 160ff.,181ff.,215ff.), who has concluded that neither city can be considered to have been an entity independent of the remaining territory of Judah and Israel. Alt exaggerated the importance of the phrase 'David and his men' in relation to the conquest of Jerusalem; this could have included the tribal armies. Moreover, in the administrative division of the territory Jerusalem is not excluded but is reckoned to belong to the tribe of Benjamin (Josh.18:28). Neither David nor his successors is ever called king of Jerusalem, which would be expected if the capital were independent, even though this title is used of pre-Israelite rulers of Jerusalem. The fact that Jerusalem is called the city of David has been adduced in favour of its independence, but in fact those Syrian city-states which really were independent entities never bore such titles. City of David is a title to be seen in the context of such titles as Gibeah of Saul, City of Nahor, Ophrah of Abiezer, and, outside the Old Testament, City of

Rameses, Fortress of Sargon. In no case is the independence of the city from the territory implied.

As far as Samaria is concerned, its purchase by Omri is not to be seen as the creation of a state within a state, nor do the letters sent by Jehu to the elders of Samaria imply such a status. Jehu's intention was the conquest of Samaria as the capital of the kingdom of Israel, and his revolt followed the normal pattern: a military coup, followed by an advance against the capital which surrendered without resistance. It is true that the title king of Samaria is to be found (1 Kings 21:1; 2 Kings 1:3), but this may derive from a time when the northern kingdom was reduced to Samaria and the territory around it, or it may have simply geographical significance, denoting the king who lives in Samaria. Dynastic kingship in Judah and Israel does not require, as Alt believed, a theory of the independence of Jerusalem and Samaria. These cities were special only in that they were the administrative, cultural and religious capitals of the respective kingdoms; they were not independent city-states.

Once again, it is probable that Alt attempted to apply an ideal type construct too rigidly to a particular historical situation, which was in reality much more complex than he allowed for. From a methodological point of view, therefore, Alt is certainly open to criticism, even though that criticism does not immediately relate to the sociological basis provided by Weber. It is to Weber's ideal type city-state that Schäfer-Lichtenberger (1983, 195ff.) has turned, in order to examine its suitability particularly for those Israelite cities on which information is available for the pre-monarchic period: Ophrah, Succoth, Penuel, Gibeah, Gilead and Jabesh. In most cases the tradition shows that they formed independent communities, not absorbed into wider societies or federations. They differed, however, from the Greek *polis* in a number of significant aspects: there was no ranking in the army and no centralized royal rule; the elders were an advisory council of representatives, while the real decision-making body was the assembly of all free independent men; there was no distinction between patricians and peasants; there was no distinction between clans with a particular clan ruling the city; there was no priesthood of local cults; society was economically and socially little differentiated. With the rise of the monarchy, these cities lost their independence. As far as the monarchic period is concerned, particularly with respect to Jerusalem and Samaria (*ibid.*,369ff.), it is clear that these cities did not constitute independent city-states within Judean and Israelite territory. Thus, the appropriateness of Weber's ideal category, built as it was largely on classical sources, is, for Schäfer-Lichtenberger, in general questionable for Israel.

The suitability of Weber's typology in this respect is not to be decided solely in relation to the question of the independence of the city-states, particularly since Weber's own description included a relationship of dependence between the city and the surrounding countryside, but rather by reference to the full range of characteristics which Weber noted. This may mean that Weber's description of the type should be modified in order better to reflect characteristics of typical Near Eastern cities rather than that it should be abandoned altogether. Significant in this regard is the study by Frick (1977), which in fact notes as typical of the ancient Near East, including Israel, a tendency towards autonomy on the part of the city (1977,174). Of particular importance, however, in developing an adequate theory of the nature of the city is Frick's use (*ibid.*,97ff.) of the typology of Sjoberg in order to distinguish clearly between the pre-industrial and the industrial city. Many of the characteristic distinctions which are drawn between the urban and the rural are typical of the industrial period but not of the pre-industrial, and so are inappropriate to the time of ancient Israel. In the Israelite context cities did not contain large resident populations; often they were simply fortified places of refuge; a considerable proportion of the city's lower class would leave the city in the morning to work as agricultural labourers. Throughout the Old Testament period the economy of the city kept its agricultural base, with little in the way of an open market economy based on trade. The city thus comprised both the city itself and its fields and villages. The city depended on its hinterland for food, while the hinterland depended on the city for a market where the agricultural produce not consumed by the farmer was offered in exchange for those few artifacts manufactured by urban specialists.

The average area of most early Israelite cities has been estimated at between five and ten acres, with a population ranging between one and three thousand. The role of urban government in the provision of services was, according to Frick (*ibid.*,114ff.), exercised by a small number of ruling families. In the early Israelite period a single extended family is found dominating a city: the Abiezrites in Ophrah, and the sons of Hamor in Shechem. Although the family remained a social unit of basic importance, in the city the elders in time came to comprise not simply the older members of families whose experience gave them authority, but rather a class founded on rank and wealth. They were the men of those families who *de facto* had the power to rule. The elders as a group could determine their own membership, in which context the ownership of real property was probably the decisive criterion. They functioned as representatives of the community in cultic and political affairs; they are associated with the leader in the exercise of his authority; they appear as a governing body; they constitute a part of the royal council; they are also a judicial body.

Urbanization increased through the monarchic period (Frick:1977,200ff.), but was inhibited by the fact that agriculture was a labour intensive activity requiring many cultivators to support even a small urban population. Israel's early social development was from a pastoral and agricultural patriarchalism to a loosely structured society of city-states; these had upper classes, and lower classes which were generally 'clients' of the upper group. With the rise of the monarchy there emerged a patrician class centred on the cities, semi-free peasants and artisan class, a patrimonial type of centralized bureaucracy, considerable market trade, and a corvée for mobilizing manpower.

Frick's description has introduced aspects of the Israelite city which may perhaps indicate the need for a shift of emphasis in Weber's description of the type, but not for a rejection of the suitability of the type for the Israelite context. In particular, the integration of the city with the countryside in pre-industrial society requires greater prominence in discussions of Israelite society, perhaps especially in the light of Gottwald's presentation of a 'dimorphic' society in Palestine (see below). Nevertheless, it may also be seen that in most vital respects the Israelite city embodies a tendency and underlying trend which strongly support its classification within the ideal type city-state as described by Weber.

4. The theoretical question of the definition of Israel and the nature of her self-understanding is difficult to answer, particularly when the biblical scheme of Israelite origins from outside the land and her consequent conquest of the land is considered to

be too simple. If no straightforward historical and ethnic distinction between Israel and other peoples can be drawn, then the basis on which Israel can now be understood, or understood herself, to be different from the Canaanites is not open to simple definition. Weber went a long way towards supplying an answer, and this, in one form or another, has appeared regularly since then (see de Geus:1976,1–68). Without raising the question of whether ultimately she came from outside the land, Weber defined Israel as a people in the land, comprising different social and economic forms, and understanding herself as a people in covenant with Yahweh. The league had a strong military aspect, and Yahweh was understood as a war god, but this did not exhaust its significance as may be seen from the Old Testament law-codes which define Israel in her relationship to Yahweh.

What was lacking in Weber, however, was provided by Noth: a definition of the institutional form through which Israel came to historical expression as the covenant people of Yahweh. Noth, through his argument that Israel in the pre-monarchic period is to be understood by analogy with the classical amphictyony, responded to the unease which was felt about making Israel's self-understanding depend simply on the idea that she was the people of Yahweh; amphictyonic Israel was the concrete form which brought that idea into life and history.

Recently, however, that theory has come under serious criticism, based on three chief grounds (Mayes:1974,15ff.; de Geus:1976,54ff.; Bächli:1977; Gottwald:1980,345ff.). First, the tribal lists on which Noth really based his view are probably much later in origin than the pre-monarchic time to which he dated them, and in any case are irrelevant to the issue of Israel's possible amphictyonic constitution: the number twelve expresses simply totality, and in the classical world the term amphictyony is used of leagues which do not have twelve members. Secondly, the historically essential characteristic of the classical amphictyony, the central sanctuary, is difficult to establish for Israel. The various criteria which have been proposed to establish the centrality of a given sanctuary in Israel (the presence of the ark, the celebration of the covenant festival, acknowledgment of the sanctuary by all Israel through its representatives) yield no unequivocal indication that any of Israel's sanctuaries had supreme importance, while her early laws, and in particular that collection, the Book of the Covenant (Ex.20:23–23:33) which has been identified as amphictyonic law, reckons with a number of local sanctuaries. Thirdly, the application of the amphictyony theory to Israel went in any case, even in Noth's original proposal, far beyond what was legitimate in the use of analogy. The amphictyony in the classical context was a cultic organization, adopted by a people already united in military and other leagues in order to maintain a balance of political and social power which had already been achieved. In the Israelite context, however, the amphictyony became a much more comprehensive institution, with social, political, ethnic and perhaps even military functions. Here Israel's political, social and ethnic consciousness was formed; at her central sanctuary the tribal representatives met and the judges functioned, and there gradually evolved there the normative account of Israelite ethnic origins which eventually found its deposit in the Pentateuch. Moreover, this amphictyony was of such fundamental significance that it survived the introduction of the monarchy and lived on as that essential Israel addressed by prophecy and law. Clearly, the amphictyony analogy has been made to bear a much too heavy weight, and even if in a more limited form it might survive, as, perhaps, a cultic institution adopted by a more limited group within Israel, it is certain that it cannot provide the answer to the question of the nature of Israel in the pre-monarchic period.

The recent study by Thiel (1980) approaches this question by going back to fundamental social issues. Though standing within the Alt-Noth framework, it brings to that approach, which otherwise has such a strong literary orientation, a broad and comprehensive sociological support. There is little in the way of sociological theory in Thiel's study, but his general approach to his topic and many detailed comments and observations indicate his adherence to the Weber tradition. The work provides a detailed account of the nature of bedouin society (on the basis of records relating to pre-Islamic Arabs and later Arab bedouin), semi-nomadism (on the basis of the Mari texts), and urban society (on the basis of the Ugaritic texts, the Alalakh tablets and the Amarna letters).

Israel's origins are thought by Thiel to lie mainly within the semi-nomadic context. In agreement with Alt, the occupation of the land is understood as a long and largely peaceful process involving in the first instance settlement of the sparsely populated mountain territory within the context of change of pasture. Thiel recognizes that there is no uniform development from a bedouin life style through semi-nomadism to settlement. Although such a development may take place, it is not relevant to Israel since the life style of the bedouin, with the camel as its economic base, is historically later than the Israelite settlement. Semi-nomadism in varying degrees of relationship with the settled way of life provides the framework for the patriarchal traditions. As in the Mari texts, so in the patriarchal traditions, this does not exclude the occasional practice of agriculture, though life was based mainly on sheep and goats, with the ass, and perhaps occasionally the camel, for transport. Property was held in common, and there was an equality to life which, after settlement, was eroded by the development of private property and the appearance of the widow, orphan, and *ger* as deprived elements in society. From pre-settlement time there derive ideas of protection for the stranger and blood revenge, together with certain cultic rituals such as Passover, the scapegoat and circumcision.

Israel's settlement is described by Thiel as a process leading from semi-nomadic pastoralism with subsidiary agriculture through a more equally distributed economic practice to a full agrarian economy with subsidiary pastoralism. In the course of this process, Israel came into (peaceful) contact with the general Canaanite farming population, which lived in the framework of a declining hierarchic city-state system. Canaanite cultural decline in the Late Bronze Age and the beginning of the Iron Age was marked by economic collapse resulting from warfare, lack of Egyptian unifying control, and anti-monarchic unrest aimed at replacing kings with a more equitable form of government. Anti-monarchism is not to be understood within an urban-rural dichotomy, for that is not true to the real character of social division in Late Bronze Age Palestine; rather, revolution was carried through by the city dwellers themselves (Thiel:1980,65ff.n.10,88ff.).

Israel's settlement is argued by Thiel to have had a gradual but fundamental effect on her social constitution: its basis in the blood related clan and family came to be replaced by territorial grouping in village communities; the clan lost its original cultic and legal functions, and the tribal institution of the elders emerged. This institution was, however, no primitive democracy; the elders exercised a limited representative role, but had no economic or political power. It was not until, and as a result of, Philistine pressure that the tribes came together under the centralized authority of the monarchy. Although there were no social classes in pre-monarchic Israel, the development of private property did bring about a growing distinction between rich and poor. Land possession was determinative, forming the basis for membership in the legal community. Through land transactions and the acquisition of large estates, together with the consolidation of the cities as seats of power by the representatives of the community, a social class of nobles emerged in the monarchic period.

That Israel was, from earliest time, of heterogeneous social composition, is acknowledged by Thiel, and is widely recognized.[7] He argues (*ibid.*,132), however, that she was also a people with a community consciousness over against the Canaanites, and that this community consciousness had a cultic sacral root, arising from common faith in Yahweh. It is just here that the fundamental problem of Israel emerges again, and it is clear that Thiel, while providing a wealth of fully documented information on social structure, has in the end not gone beyond Weber in resolving that problem. 'Israel' is to be found somehow within these different social forms. The amphictyony analogy, however, has proved inappropriate for this context and purpose, but one must, Thiel concludes, understand some institutional form for the expression of this common faith, which gave Israel a sense of community despite territorial, social and economic divisions.

5. Alt and Noth largely determined the extent to which use was made of Weber in the study of ancient Israel. It is all the more necessary, therefore, to refer to two recent studies in the tradition of Weber which fall outside the Alt–Noth framework. The first of these is by Fishbane and the second by Otto.
a. It has already been noted (above,20ff.) that Weber described three ideal types of authority: charismatic, traditional and legal-rational. These can be seen to be interrelated in two ways. In the first place, by a process of routinization charismatic authority may become traditional and eventually legal-rational. Secondly, in so far as these are ideal types and not empirical forms, any given structure of authority will normally embody more than one of these types; no historical expression of authority is ever purely charismatic or traditional or legal-rational.

Corresponding to these different types of authority there are also ideal types of law making. In *Ancient Judaism* (84,87) Weber both noted that law arises first through oracular responses from charismatics, and also referred to law which has been given a rational formulation. The background to this kind of allusion is to be found in his comprehensive study (1954), in which he discussed charismatic law making, the empirical creation of *ad hoc* laws, the imposition and systematization of laws, and the systematic, theoretical elaboration of laws, as four ideal types of law making. These are clearly to be linked, more or less directly, with the types of authority, and, like the latter, may be understood as interrelated types. On the one hand, the four types belong on a continuum in which law making becomes an increasingly rational activity. On the other hand, these ideal types of law making, like the ideal types of authority, may be anchored in typical social contexts: the first two in patriarchal and tribal type societies, the third and fourth in an increasingly bureaucratized state. Such social structures, however, are never purely one type or another, and so the different forms of authority and forms of law making will, on the empirical level, also be found together.

At least three of the four types of law making are to be found, as Fishbane (1985,234ff.) has recognized, in the Old Testament. Charismatic law making, which is the form implied when reference is made to oracular consultation, is associated on several occasions with Moses, who, in the cases of the blasphemer (Lev.24:18–23), the Sabbath breaker (Nu.15:32–36), and the inheritance rights of the daughters of Zelophehad (Nu. 27:1–11), reached a decision only after enquiring of God. The empirical creation of law is found in David's judgment, against traditional practice, that all soldiers should receive an equal share in the spoils of war (1 Sam.30:22–5), and in Solomon's famous decision in the case of the mothers contending over a child (1 Kings 3:16–28). The imposition and systematization of laws by secular or theocratic powers is to be associated with the rational systematizing of bureaucratic organization in a developing society. This activity is reflected in Moses' appointment of judges and his reservation to himself of difficult cases (Deut.1:17), and in the reference to the study and teaching of the law of Yahweh by Ezra (Ezra 7:10). The fourth form of law making relates to the formulation of highly abstract rules, usually within the

framework of study and exegesis in law schools. There is little
sign of this in the Old Testament, unless the tendency to regard
all the commandments as of equal weight (as in Nu.15:22 – 31)
be understood to presuppose that degree of abstract reflection.

Again, following Weber, the status of these forms as ideal types
must be recognized; the continuum of types cannot be understood
to imply that all Old Testament examples of, for example,
charismatic law making are necessarily historically older than
other forms. The involvement of priests alongside judges in
judicial decision making (Deut.17:8ff.) presupposes that
charismatic (oracular) law making was not replaced by but existed
alongside the more rational modes as they developed.

b. In a recent study, Otto (1988) has proposed a detailed
redactional history of the Book of the Covenant (Ex.20 – 23), and,
in setting this within the framework of social developments in
Israel, has reached conclusions of fundamental significance for
the history of the development of Israelite law. Israelite law, he
has argued, did not develop through a process of increasing
secularization; rather, it came increasingly to be grounded in
the will of Yahweh. This theological process is linked with, and
is a continuation of, social developments bringing about social
stratification, for the divisions in society that resulted from the
disparity between rich and poor meant that the unity of society
itself no longer existed as a motivation and legitimation of law.
This lack of motivation for law became an issue in the first
instance in relation to laws dealing with those who are at the
edge of society: the poor, the widow, the orphan, the alien, and
the slave; so it is in relation to laws dealing with them that
religious motivations begin to make their appearance. From this
point the process developed its own dynamic, resulting in the
incorporation of wider spheres of Israelite life under the rule of
Yahweh. The process culminated in the deuteronomistic
interpretation of the Book of the Covenant, through which it
was incorporated into the Sinai pericope as an expression of the
will of Yahweh for his covenant people.

This process may be seen in the chiastic structures of both
major units of the Book of the Covenant (Ex.21:2 – 22:26;
22:27 – 23:12). In the first, the reparation laws of 21:33 – 22:14
combine simple restoration laws regulating conflict between equal
families with laws which include a punishment; the former reflect
a tribal society, the latter a state in which authority is used to

maintain a hierarchical social system. The slave law in Ex. 21:2–11 corresponds to the concluding section of the chiastic unit in Ex.22:20–26 in dealing with the disadvantaged in society and also in the theological foundation which is either implicit (in the requirement that the slave should be freed in the seventh year) or explicit in the laws. Laws which originally depended on a sense of social identity for their justification and motivation are here strengthened by being made an expression of the divine will. This transformation of law into an ethical requirement sets the context within which all the laws of the unit are to be understood.

A parallel development may be seen in the second unit, Ex. 22:27–23:12. The laws on legal procedures in Ex.23:1–3,6–8, which show a history of development in reaction to the threat to legal procedures posed by the emergence of concentrated economic power in the eighth century, have been edited to make Yahweh their source. Moreover, the redactor of the unit has structured them around an ethical demand, the requirement for help for one's enemy (Ex.23:4f.), and has created a framework in Ex.22:28f.; 23:10–12, which expresses the idea of the sovereignty of God as that which puts a limit on man's disposal over nature.

When both units were set together the Book of Covenant was created, with an outer framework in Ex.21:2–11; 23:10–12 and an inner framework in Ex.22:20–26; 22:28f., which required protection for the weak and poor and put a religious restriction on man's use of nature and of other men. This combination of social protection law and sacral law became the governing theological outlook of the whole collection. The deuteronomistic redactor, at work in Ex.20:22f.; 23:13–33, continued the development by presenting the collection as a covenant law for a restored community, in which cult and daily life are brought together in a new Israel.

The complex history of the Book of the Covenant reflects, at first, social developments in which Israel became a hierarchical state with concerns which could not be met by the old casuistic conflict law. In particular, the appearance of a sanction in casuistic law, and its combination with old family apodictic law which already had a sanction, reflects a centralizing process in which the administration of law became a means by which the hierarchic state was maintained. With increasing social diversity, social identity and community could no longer of itself motivate law, particularly law dealing with the protection of the disadvantaged, and so it is in relation to such laws that the theologizing of the law began. In this development, law found a foundation in a theological dimension transcending empirical society: the more society suffered from its divisions, the stronger it expressed its unity from Yahweh. This theological development has transformed the law into ethical preaching. So the legal history of Israel is a history of integration of the law into the divine will: from a socio-historical perspective, this is the result of crisis in legal motivation and legitimation arising from social diversity; from a religious perspective, it is the result of an increasingly explicit universality of the rule of God over the daily life of Israel.

This highly significant study stands strongly in the tradition of Weber. It reflects a development from Weber which is, however, somewhat out of line with the form which Weber's approach assumed in the work of Noth. Whereas the latter came to propose a concrete social structure for the religiously grounded Israel which Weber described, in the work of Otto this religiously grounded Israel is a religious proposition carried along within the context of empirical social developments to which it does not precisely correspond. The extent to which this reflects also Weber's view depends on how the latter is interpreted; but it certainly conforms in a general way with Weber's understanding of the relationship between religion and society. Otto has, however, at least supplemented, if not modified, Weber in arguing that the early stages of the Book of the Covenant, particularly its old casuistic law and family apodictic law, reflect an Israelite society whose unity lay in the co-ordination of the equal families in its tribal structure, rather than in a common commitment to Yahweh overriding social and economic disparity.

It may be that Otto (1988, 94 n.229) has dismissed too quickly the possibility that from the beginning law had an implicit religious foundation in that it was understood to derive from a religious world order, so that he has left a too narrow space and too restricted function for religion in ancient society. This, however, does not affect his argument that the incorporation of the explicit religious motivation, to which Weber appealed as an indication of the covenant foundation of Israel, reflects a transfer of the law out of the context of the administration of justice and into the context of ethical preaching. The Israel which is addressed by such preaching is then not a covenant community within the framework of which Israel originated, but a hierarchic state whose social structure stands in considerable tension with the ideal presupposed in such preaching.

Israelite religion and society in the conflict tradition

1. If Weber is to be seen simply as an idealist, then there are several studies of Israelite religion and society which may be included within the framework of the tradition to which he belongs. This would be true especially of the work of Mendenhall, noted in the first chapter, but it would also apply to the work of Bright (cf. Gottwald:1980,592ff.). For the latter, the only unique thing about Israel was her religion: only this marked Israel off as distinctive (Bright:1981,144). The religion of Israel was, therefore, an idea quite independent of the history and social system of Israel. This represents, however, a form of idealism which, it should already be clear, is not true to Weber or the conflict tradition; it stands at the opposite extreme to the historical materialism which indeed Weber vehemently opposed, but is in the end as one-sided and, to Weber, unrealistic as that historical materialism.

Closer to Weber is the attempt of Fohrer (1971; 1973,23ff.) to describe the influence of Israel's historical experience and social structure on her expression of her faith. So, Israel's nomadic origins are the background of her conception of God as associated with a group rather than with a place; from this same context derive the traditions of divine promise of land and posterity, the Passover festival, the tent and ark, and certain laws, especially those dealing with marriage relationships. Israel's adoption of the settled and agricultural way of life led to a conception of Yahweh as the God of rain and fruitfulness, while the adoption of a monetary economy and the development of economic class distinctions in society are the background of prophetic preaching. Fohrer argues that these social factors determined the expression and certain features of the faith of Israel in particular times; they do not, however, account for its totality. There are certain essential elements of Israelite faith, which remain determinative in all its various social and historical manifestations, and which are not to be derived from social and historical circumstances: these include the personal nature of Israelite faith which is found in even its earliest manifestation, the idea of the acts of God in individual and national lives, the demand that life be lived according to God's will (Fohrer:1973,24). Thus, in particular, the prophets and their defence of the rights of the deprived are not open to sociological explanation; the reasons for their appearance, from a sociological point of view, are not open to us.

Fohrer is undoubtedly right both to point to aspects of Israelite religion which are expressions of her social circumstances, and also to break any essential relationship of direct correspondence between religious belief and social circumstances. Yet, by failing to explore other approaches to the question of the sources of religious belief he leaves himself open to the charge of idealism, that he has reserved, in an arbitrary way, an essential core of religious belief from historical and sociological enquiry. In particular, Fohrer's account assumes a paradigm according to which the religious belief of society, however fundamentally shaped by social convention, comes under the criticism of, and is ultimately reformed by, individuals (prophets) who are somehow free of these conventions. The pattern is too simple and monolithic, and takes no account either of the interaction in society of different groups with different sets of conventions or of the formation of religious beliefs and ideas within an ongoing diachronic historical framework as opposed to a synchronic social framework.

2. This more complex picture, which is truer to Weber and the conflict tradition, is better represented in two studies by Otto. The first (1976) is concerned with the relationship between cult and politics in the creation of the Davidic state as a political structure in which Canaanites, independently of the Israelite tribes, acknowledged David as overlord. The nature of the problem emerges when David's policy of integration is contrasted with that of Saul who tried to destroy the Canaanite population. Otto argues that behind these very different political policies there lie contrasting cultic traditions, that of Gilgal on the one hand and that of Shiloh on the other. The Gilgal tradition of Yahwism is the nationalistic Israelite tradition of Saul; David's having Abiathar as priest and his bringing of the ark to Jerusalem establish his relationship with the Shiloh tradition. The Shiloh tradition of the worship of Yahweh was characterized by festivals (dancing in the vineyards), symbols (the lamp of God, the ephod) and a temple, which have close connections with Canaanite forms of worship. This cult tradition thus provided the basis, which the Gilgal tradition could not supply, for David's political policy of integrating Canaanites with Israelites in the one state.

Otto's second contribution (1981) has enlarged on this same approach. Here it is argued that religion and social integration are closely related, in the sense that the understanding of God takes up and is shaped by that which serves as the central integrating element of society. Thus, patriarchal society is limited to the family as the basic legal, economic and religious community. The function of the family father as leader and protector of that community is taken up into the understanding of God. Religion is transcendent only within the limits of the family and can provide no basis for society going beyond the family; patriarchal religion could not become the religion of Israel, because it would not relate to the daily experience of a social unit greater than the family. The formation of a more complex society of families and tribes after settlement required a different form of religious integration, one which was provided by Yahweh, the wilderness God of Sinai who was not bound by the limits of the family but was essentially related to human solidarity expressed in ethical integration. The ability of Yahwism to function in the integration of the daily experience of Israel was, however, limited by the fact that Yahweh had no connection to fertility and the farming life; this lack was made good in the cult of Shiloh where, in the taking up of mythical elements into the religion of Israel, Yahweh came to be worshipped as king, creator and lord of nature. Religion integrates social-political experiences and needs; it then works back upon society creating the possibility of the existence of a tribal egalitarian society rather than a patriarchal society, and then of a state hierarchical society rather than a tribal egalitarian society.

It is this aspect of religion, its transcending the limitations imposed by the political and social circumstances of its adherents, which is basic to the distinction drawn by Miller (1976) between religion as faith and religion as ideology. Admitting the presence of ideological as opposed to faith elements in Israelite religion, Miller defines ideology as a selective and partial interpretation of a society's circumstances, which reflects the need of a group to identify and justify its goals (Miller:1976,466). Ideological expressions in the Old Testament are particularly the idea of a chosen people and of divine promises directed to that people. Faith is distinguished from ideology by three criteria: the presence of self-criticism; a positive relationship with other peoples in the sense that Israel's place in the world is not defined solely in terms of its own particular interests; the demand for justice and righteousness in human conduct. These criteria determine the presence of a critique of the ideological interest in supporting and maintaining the group.

The early poetry of the Old Testament, for example Exodus 15 and Judges 5, is dominated by ideological factors: Israel is the people of Yahweh who defeats all her enemies and leads her in conquest of the promised land; Yahweh's interests and those of Israel are identical. The Yahwist also expresses an ideology in terms of providing a theological basis for the unity of Israel in her land by telling of divine promises to her ancestors. On the other hand, the Yahwist goes beyond this by presenting Israel as the channel of divine blessing to the world, a theme which is in fact the end and goal of blessing on Israel herself. This, along with the demand for justice and righteousness in human conduct, found in the story of Abraham's intercession for Sodom (Gen.18:19), expresses a critique of nationalistic pride and checks the dominance of ideological factors in Israelite religion. The deuteronomistic account of the conquest represents in some measure an ideological elaboration of actual practice, a justification of the way in which Israel secured the land: Israel is the chosen people, to whom the land was given as the gift of Yahweh. Yet in Deuteronomy itself there is a mixture of faith and ideology, especially in so far as Israel is warned not to assume that it was because of her goodness or greatness that she was given the land (Deut.9:4ff.). The implicit critique of ideology which is present here is brought out strongly by the prophets. The background of their appearance is a state ideology which emphasized the divine promise to the Davidic dynasty (Pss.89;132), with only a minor role being played by the demand for obedience to the divine will. The prophets criticized this ideological distortion; it was their function to destroy the identification of faith with ideology, something they could do because they were outside the institutions of power (Miller:1976,474). Amos's criticism of the old election tradition (3:2), Jeremiah's denunciation of popular security based on the temple (7:3), and Second Isaiah's universalism, all stand in continuity with but transcend the old national ideology of the chosen people in her land.

This is a valuable study which brings the sociological issue right to the centre of the study of Israelite religion. It may, however, be seen as too apologetic in its approach, particularly in that it takes its starting point in Karl Mannheim's argument that all human thought is subject to the influence of its social context. If this is so, then the validity of the criteria for distinguishing faith from ideology must be carefully examined, for it could well be argued that no thought can be claimed in any absolute way to belong to the realm of faith rather than that of ideology.[8] Uncertainty about Miller's general approach is, moreover, strengthened by his suggestion (*ibid.*,465) that the term ideology does not have to imply a value judgment, for the distinction which he then proceeds to make between faith and ideology does carry precisely this implication. Faith is human thought and belief which is free of the social and economic interests which limit ideology. Faith is understood to be that which is uncontaminated by material interests.

On the other hand, none of the criteria proposed by Miller necessarily distinguish faith from ideology. As far as universalism and the demand for justice and righteousness are concerned, these are characteristic elements of what may be called a royal ideology. The king's task of administering justice and righteousness, of caring for the poor and outcast, is the regular content of a rationale of kingship which is aimed at preserving the status quo: the present conditions are part of the divine plan in creation, and it is the function of the king to maintain and promote them (cf. Stolz:1973,147ff.). On this basis, universalism and the demand for justice and righteousness may, in Miller's terms, be clearly judged to be ideological rather than characteristics of faith. The criterion of self-judgment is likewise open to ideological understanding, for that expression, which may be traced to a prophetic or charismatic critique of the pretensions of royal power, may be held to derive not from an ideal setting free of the influences of its social context, but from an ideology alternative to that held by those criticized.

This whole enterprise may, as Miller indeed admits (*ibid.*,477 n.10), be ultimately impossible: the ideological and theological represent attitudes towards, and perspectives on, the same sets of ideas, rather than clear distinctions between ideas in any objective sense (see also Anderson:1985,292ff.).

3. Some recent developments in the study of Israelite religion are by no means incompatible with the foregoing. It has been strongly argued by Lang (1983) that the development of Israelite monotheism is to be seen in terms of the eventual success of the programme of an active pressure group within Israel which, particularly in times of crisis, came to dominance. Yahweh was one God worshipped among others for much of Israel's pre-exilic

history: besides the various El deities referred to in the patriarchal stories, Baal was worshipped in a temple in Jerusalem during the monarchic period (2 Kings 11:18) and other alien gods were acknowledged in the temple of Yahweh (Ezek.8), while Ashera (2 Kings 23:7) and the Queen of Heaven (Jer.44:25) were also officially recognized. The course by which Yahweh alone became God of Israel was a historical and social one, the major steps of which may be fairly clearly discerned. Israel at first, as its name implies, worshipped El. It was the achievement of that group of slaves which identified its escape from Egypt as the deliverance of Yahweh, to coalesce with underprivileged groups in Palestine, and, on the basis of the common experience of insecurity and oppression, to identify El, the God of Israel, with Yahweh. This was a move which took place in a situation of crisis and catastrophe, a situation comparable, in terms of the threat which it posed to the lives of people, to that which later obtained on several occasions during the monarchic period: first, as Solomon sought to bring Israel into a new state of servitude, then as Jezebel attempted to impose her own Phoenician culture and religion on the land, and, most catastrophically, as the Assyrians and later the Babylonians destroyed first Israel and then Judah. The breakthrough to monotheism was achieved only in the framework of that final catastrophe, when the historical demand for the worship of Yahweh alone, with its threat of punishment for disobedience, was finally vindicated. Israelite religious development is thus to be seen not simply in terms of the evolution of theological ideas, but rather also in terms of the conflict of competing ideologies within specific historical and social circumstances.

4. In this context, the understanding of the figure of the prophet is crucial, for here, it seems, lies the focus for that process, both social and theological, by which the worship of Yahweh was brought to that point of exclusiveness which the Old Testament presupposes for the whole of Israel's existence. In other words, the prophet was not simply the isolated source of new religious ideas but rather the focal point of social and religious movements by which such ideas became established in Israel.

In a discussion of the significance of the term authority, when used of the prophets, Long (1977,3ff.), strongly echoing the Weber type of approach, identifies prophetic authority as a social reality. Behind the Old Testament theological presentation of the prophet as called by God or speaking with divine authority, there lies a social reality, a relationship of domination and subordination, which is accepted as legitimate. It is a highly unstable situation in which the legitimacy of the prophet's claim was open to and required public validation; this was provided through such things as the fulfilment of signs and prophecies and the conformity of the prophet to the role expected of him. The authority of the prophet became real only in so far as it was accepted by others; authority, like charisma, is a term of social relationship.

In general, however, the term charisma has been avoided in the discussion of prophecy. The reason for this is perhaps in part to be found in a problem within Weber's presentation of the prophet, noted especially by Petersen (1979,132ff.; cf. also Wilson:1980,56ff.). Weber described the prophet as an individual bearer of charisma, marked out from other religious functionaries by his personal call, a free speaker proclaiming revelations in vital emotional preaching (Weber:1965,46f.). The prophet proclaimed, under the influence of spontaneous inspiration, and with complete inner independence, to the public in the market place or to the elders at the city gate. The spirit came on the prophet in solitude; through hearing the voice of God, the prophet was assured of his function as the tool of Yahweh (Weber:1952,271ff.,291ff.). This presentation of the solitary prophet is difficult to reconcile with his description as a charismatic, for the essence of Weber's understanding of charisma is that it denotes a relationship between a leader and his followers. Weber's description of the solitariness of the classical prophets, a description which may in fact owe much to the Wellhausen school's portrayal of the prophet as a solitary and free opponent of the priesthood, leaves too little room for a charismatic relationship between the prophet and his followers.

Petersen's belief, however, that Weber has confused two ideal types, the type of the prophet and the type of the charismatic, and that these should be distinguished, is probably a too drastic solution to this problem. It involves the danger of accepting too uncritically the notion of the prophet as a socially detached voice of protest. That such a view of the prophet is potentially distorting may be illustrated by reference first to Berger's study (1963) of the relationship between charisma and office, and, secondly, to

Overholt's discussion (1982) of the question of the social location of prophecy.

Berger notes that Weber's general theory of the nature of charismatic leadership was, in fact, largely based on his understanding of the pre-exilic prophets, and sets out to examine how that theory might then be affected by developments in the understanding of prophecy since then. Weber's view of prophecy was significantly influenced by Wellhausen and his followers: classical prophecy is rooted in ecstatic Nabiism, which manifested itself in the context of peasant warfare; as a result of the demilitarization of the peasantry, prophecy became in the first instance institutionalized court prophecy, but in the ninth century there emerged a new form of prophetic opposition, on behalf of traditional Yahwism, to the innovations of the monarchy. In this development, the prophets became socially detached, concerned with ethics rather than cult, and interpreters of the political history who helped ensure that Yahwism survived the exile. In this understanding, Weber reflected the standard nineteenth and early twentieth century Protestant interpretation of classical prophecy as an anti-cultic protest movement (cf. also Lang:1984,158ff.). More recently, especially as a result of the work of Mowinckel, Johnson, Haldar, Würthwein and Gunneweg, this picture has been fundamentally modified: form criticism has shown the dependence of prophetic literature on material derived from the cult; the cult was much more central to all aspects of life and left more room for a prophetic type of spirituality than was formerly believed. The result, according to Berger, is that it is now widely, if not generally, accepted that the classical prophets were strongly rooted in the cultic tradition of Israel, that they differed from the Nabis not in terms of their office but in terms of the radical understanding which they brought to it. Proclamations of judgment were common to all; the classical prophets push these to the extreme point of suggesting that Yahweh might abandon Israel. This, however, is a distinction in theology, and does not imply that from a sociological point of view they stood outside the office to which the Nabis also belonged. The radicalization of the classical prophets came from within rather than from without.

If this is so, then Weber's understanding of the individuality of the classical prophets must be modified, by breaking down the traditional opposition of prophet and priestly office. These prophets too belonged to an office, a charismatic office, as part of the cultic institution. This is a modification to Weber's understanding of prophecy, but it in fact strengthens his description of charisma, for while the non-traditional and non-rational aspects of this form of authority are not to be denied, it is not to be thought of in an idealistic and wholly individualistic way. It is a power for radical change deriving from within the institutions of society rather than from outside those institutions (Berger:1963,950); it belongs in society rather than outside society, and remains essentially a term of relationship for that irrational and non-traditional influence which the leader exerts on his followers.

Berger's study has usefully drawn attention to the centrality of the cult in Israelite society, and warned against a too narrow definition of its function; it has also indicated how the innovatory power of charisma does not necessarily imply social marginality.[9] In so far, however, as it could also lead to a too diffuse understanding of cult and an imprecise understanding of the basic element in Weber's description of charisma, that it is a term of relationship, it should be supplemented by reference to a recent study by Overholt which proposes a modification in the form by which the function of a prophet in society is to be understood (Overholt:1982,55ff.). The normal model, according to which the prophet mediates to Israel a message received from God, presents both prophet and people as passive recipients of a divine word and takes no account of the social and political context out of which that word came and into which it was spoken, nor does it reckon with the already existing access which the people has to the word of God in the cult independently of the prophet. Moreover, such a linear model of prophecy makes it very difficult to comprehend and accommodate the phenomenon of prophetic conflict, as described in Jeremiah 28, except by imposing on such situations the later anachronistic categories of 'true prophet' and 'false prophet'. In Overholt's view, however, these problems are largely resolved if our model of prophecy is changed to a triangular one in which the prophet interacts with both God and people, and in which the people have their own relationship with God apart from the prophetic channel of communication. Thus, both prophet and people become together active participants in a process by which the word of God comes to expression, a word which is to be understood not simply as a divine gift but as the expression of the will of God which is realized for a particular group through its interaction with the prophet.

For Overholt, therefore, the word of God comes into being in the relationship of the prophet with others. In so far as this word is recognized as word of God, it may be said that the prophet articulates what is recognized as word of God by those who, independent of the prophet, have an expectation, even if unformulated, of the nature of that word (cf. also Long: 1977,3ff.). So, the disciples of Isaiah constitute a support group in interaction with whom Isaiah articulates the word of God, a word which he can then carry to those outside who are perhaps inimical and unreceptive to what he has to say. It is, therefore, understandable how prophetic conflict could arise: prophets and their disciples belong to different social and political contexts of society, and it is in part these very social and political differences which come to expression in that conflict. It is wrong to think in terms of the prophet simply as the complete outsider; this would imply that his words found no receptive echo in the minds of his audience, and this would necessarily have led to his being ignored and forgotten. The existence of the collections of prophetic oracles testifies to the existence of those who were receptive to the prophetic words, and it is in the prophet's charismatic relationship with them, whether a closely defined support group or not, that the divine word came to expression.

These two complementary studies, by Berger and Overholt, may thus be held to modify very considerably the presentation of the classical prophets as socially detached and isolated individuals. Not only were they strongly related to the cult, but their word of God reflects a close interaction between the prophet and his disciples. In this light, it is then wholly appropriate to continue Weber's use of the term charismatic, understood as a term of relationship, for the classical prophets, even if Weber's somewhat inconsistent tendency to emphasize the independence of the classical prophets should be appropriately revised.

4

The Structural-functionalist Tradition in Old Testament Study

Antonin Causse

Introduction
In this chapter reference is made to works in which the influence of Durkheim may be clearly traced, and to others which only in general terms may be argued to lie within the structural-functionalist tradition which Durkheim founded. Some of the latter are characterized by an emphasis on the materialist approach to history or the materialist basis of Israelite history, with which Durkheim would not have agreed, but their inclusion in this context is justified by their view of society as a structured unit, by their understanding of historical change as the result of the disruption of the balance in the structure, and especially by their tendency to eliminate the human subject as the active agent of social relationships and of social change. In all these respects there is a clear reflection of Durkheim's understanding of society and of the relationship of the individual to society.

Durkheim did not write on ancient Israel; his influence, however, and that of his associates, is to be clearly traced in the work of many of those who did. A contemporary in France, closely associated with his sociological approach, was Lévy-Bruhl (Parsons:1944,181ff.; Evans-Pritchard:1965,78ff.; Rogerson: 1978,46ff.). He, like Durkheim, distinguished between primitive and civilized human societies, and, again like Durkheim, considered that the mentality of the individual derived from the collective representations of his society which impose themselves on him. Lévy-Bruhl, however, went on to probe the nature of the mentality of those who constituted primitive societies, and attempted to maintain the sociological approach by arguing that the patterns of thought which he described were social facts, the collective representations of society held by all members of the society. Primitive mentality he described as pre-logical, in the sense of being unscientific and uncritical; it does not distinguish between the natural and the supernatural, nor between subject and object. All are bound together in a mystical network of relationships. Primitive mentality sees all beings and objects as sharing in the same nature (Lévy-Bruhl:[1927]1965,19). There is a general kinship of plant and animal life, within the framework of which human individual identity is often merged with that of the animal or plant from which he is thought to have derived (*ibid.*,50). The totemic ancestor, either animal or plant, is the mystic essence in which is expressed the identity of the social group.

Lévy-Bruhl intended this as a sociological account of primitive mentality; these mystical relationships were collective representations of society. His approach was, however, open to being understood in solely psychological terms, which would imply a reversal of the direction in which the theory was supposed to go: social structures could be seen as based upon and reflections of primitive forms of thought. It was in such terms that it was taken up by Wheeler Robinson and his followers in their theory of 'corporate personality' (cf. Rogerson:1970,1ff.). By using Lévy-Bruhl in this way, it was hoped to provide a psychological confirmation, in terms of the innate structure of primitive human consciousness, for the apparent psychic unity of the group presupposed by certain Old Testament passages, such as the Achan story of Joshua 7. The theory of corporate personality in ancient Israel has, however, come under attack, in relation to both the exegesis of those passages which were held to reflect it (Porter:1965,361ff.) and the understanding of primitive mentality derived from Lévy-Bruhl (Rogerson: *ibid.*); indeed, Lévy-Bruhl's general sociological theory has also been seriously questioned (Parsons:1944,181ff.; Evans-Pritchard:1965,78ff.). Before these criticisms appeared, however, a synthesis of Durkheim and Lévy-Bruhl within the distinctive French school of sociology, along with the work of Robertson Smith on which Durkheim relied, had become the fruitful basis of a number of Old Testament studies by Antonin Causse.

Religion and society in ancient Israel

Causse was not a sociologist, and his work cannot be considered to have a sociological significance comparable to that of Weber. Nevertheless, as the first expounder of the Old Testament and ancient Israel within his consciously adopted sociological framework, he may be seen to have performed for Old Testament scholarship a service parallel to that of Weber. Weber's *Ancient Judaism* is an expression of the conflict tradition in sociology as it relates to Israel; Causse's *Du groupe ethnique à la communauté religieuse*, which is dedicated to Lévy-Bruhl, is an expression of the structural-functionalist tradition in sociology as it relates to Israel (see further Kimbrough:1972; 1978).

In this work Causse, being chiefly concerned with the transition in Israelite religion and society from the primitive pre-logical mentality, where religion is scarcely different from magic, to the rationalism and individualism basic to later ethical conceptions, attempted to integrate the evolutionary approach of Reuss, Graf and Wellhausen with French sociology. His approach and the very structure of his study are, therefore, fundamentally different from those of Weber. Weber, indeed, is criticized for not having taken adequate account of the primitive structure of the mentality of ancient Israelites: Weber's teleological approach, which set at the beginning the question how Israel became a pariah people, led him to transpose into antiquity the conditions of a much later and more developed time (Causse:1973,9).

Causse understood early Israel to have carried over from its nomadic past a social structure consisting of families, clans and tribes. Settlement involved a certain weakening in the old kinship constitution of society, with territorial groupings tending to replace kinship groups, and primitive collectivism, in which all things were held in common, being replaced by the concept of the family land, which from then on was to form the corner-stone of Israelite society. Family and clan structures, however, were strongly maintained: the father had supreme authority in the family, while in the clan the elders represented the 'living soul' which realized the unity of the group. The group was characterized by 'organic solidarity':[1] there was no individual differentiation; the individual existed only in absolute dependence on the whole and in the context of the whole. The relationship of the group is a mystical community of soul, which comes to expression in certain rituals of brotherhood; it is a covenant relationship, established by eating together, exchanging clothes or arms; those united in the group form a physico-psychic unity. Any weakening in this bond resulting from settlement was compensated for by an even more binding unity constituted by the common worship of Yahweh. Community in the worship of Yahweh was achieved especially through sacrifice, which established a mystic kinship relationship with the god. The cult, which was simple and spontaneous, was the most powerful of socially binding influences and the foundation of the solidarity of the group: the tribes formed a federation under the leadership of Yahweh, who was worshipped not simply as a God of war but also as the God of Israelite society, the guardian of tribal custom, defender of the weak and the poor, who punishes the guilty.

The introduction of the monarchy and urbanization, although not displacing the patriarchal system, especially in outlying areas, did have critical effects on the old solidarities. Cities became the centres and villages dependent on them; the social centre of gravity was thus shifted towards what were inherently unstable social structures. Already existing differences between rich and poor developed into class differences, as a result of which rich and poor now lived separate lives. As the authority of the state interposed itself in the lives of Israelites, so the authority of the family father declined. The traditional laws of redemption, levirate marriage and help for the widow and orphan became weaker and a system of compensation for wrong began to develop. This signified a growth of individual responsibility and so also a crisis with regard to the old solidarity.

In effect, the mystical bond holding together the social group was under attack and losing its ancient power. The monarchy, as the centre of the unity of the people and its source of life and prosperity, had its own mystical base. Yahweh became the God of the state, universal God, rather than the God of the tribe; a professional priesthood and foreign cults emerged. Thus, the cult became separated from the life of the primitive group, and the simple, joyful, natural worship of the family grouped around its patron God declined. The ancient rituals lost their efficacy, rites of penitence and purification came to be emphasized, and the old natural intimacy between the worshipper and his God was lost. Into this setting of social and religious dislocation came the prophets with their proclamation of a new society and a new covenant bond.

Prophecy and the deuteronomic reform

Prophecy appeared with the foundation of the monarchy, but took vigorous form in the northern kingdom in the time of the Omrides. These prophets were at the head of a conservative reaction against a secular state founded on force, which had no links with old Israel; it is a reaction reflected also in the Yahwist, the laws of the book of the covenant and the decalogues. There is expressed here no romantic idealization of the desert, but rather the wish to restore the old culture and patriarchal organization of the simple peasantry, without king or professional priesthood and systematic cult. Authority should be exercised by the family father and elders, and the old covenant relationship of the social group should be expressed in a cult at a simple altar.

For the later eighth-century prophets, however, the golden age was the nomadic life far from the seductions of cult and idolatry. With settlement Israel's life had become corrupted by human works and proud reliance on human strength. The idea that all human work is profane and that to rely on it is sin against God reflects primitive mysticism; the ardent faith of the classical prophets, their demand to trust only in Yahweh, belong to a pre-logical mentality. Whatever they may have intended, however, with their proclamation of the mystical values of the past, the prophets effectively destroyed the old tribal and clan ways. By condemning the local sanctuaries and their cults, they condemned the very places where the clans and families had realized their social unity in cultic song and festival. The prophets indeed shared with popular religion the sense of the solidarity of the group with its God, but they did not conceive of this solidarity as a mystical-magical connection established and renewed by cultic communal rites; instead, they gave it an ethical foundation, righteousness.

The law had long been considered to have divine origin, divine guarantee and sanction, an idea already found in the Hammurabi Code and in the conception of Maat in Egypt; with the prophets of Israel the new thing is their subjective determination of what in ancient rite and custom should be maintained and what should be abandoned. The mystic magic of the cult is rejected as a means of maintaining the covenant; morality is the indispensable condition of right relations with God. This struck at the very basis of ancient society, for the existence and prosperity of which the cult had fundamental significance. In moralizing and rationalizing the cult, the prophets opened the way to an individualistic conception of religion and social organization. By spiritualizing and interiorizing religion they promoted a piety which became more and more personal. The institutions of collective life and national religion came to have only a secondary importance. Probably with some debt to Weber, Causse referred to the work of the eighth and seventh century prophets as that of rationalizing the religious tradition and the social institutions. Thus was accomplished the transition from primitive collectivism to moral individualism.

The seventh century deuteronomic reform movement was an attempt to resolve the crisis provoked by the prophets, by putting a brake on the decline of ancient social organization. To this end, Deuteronomy is a restatement of ancient laws, rites and institutions, though with modifications and adaptations which betray the critical situation to which it is addressed. The family father has lost a lot of his social and religious authority; the elders are still important but they share their functions with the Levites (the significance of the latter indicating a process of social transformation from clan society to church). The old tribal organization has lost its base; it is the assembly of the people which represents the supreme organ of the nation, not the elders or leaders. The king is no longer transcendent, an indispensable intermediary between God and man, but one of the brethren; it is on the people as a whole that responsibility rests for prosperity or distress, not on the leaders. Through laws regulating remission of debts and slavery, Deuteronomy intends to restore a balance to Israelite society, and specifically to re-establish the class of small peasantry, threatened with slavery or with being confined to a proletariat class by the development of the *latifundia.*

On the other hand, the deuteronomic lawgiver does not expect the covenant law to be obeyed simply because it is old; society has lost its ancient solidarity and people no longer unquestioningly accept what they have received from the past. The deuteronomic lawgiver must persuade his hearers with exhortations, explanations and rational motives. The covenant which had earlier rested on the mystical foundation of eating together or the sprinkling of blood, now rests on law which is taught. The law on centralization has separated the sacred from everyday life; ordinary life has now become profane, and out of it the individual must be persuaded to become, through obedience to the law, a member of the people of Yahweh.

Causse has seen here a distinct advance on what was still the pre-logical mentality of the prophets. The old mystical authority and unity of the social group is now gone, and is to be replaced by rational authority and community based on a moral order which individuals are persuaded to obey. Parenesis is characteristic of Deuteronomy. The blessings and curses have lost their magical roots and depend upon a logical, rational relationship between justice and blessing, injustice and distress. Old laws, which originally had a magical or mystical basis, are now given rational motivations. This new rationalizing spirit had the effect of contributing to the crisis precipitated by prophetic preaching. By trying to rationalize the old law, the deuteronomic legislator introduced into the sacred domain of ancestral tradition the destructive element of individual reflection. He shook the authority of ancestral custom and substituted exhortation and voluntary compliance. In place of the old physico-mystical solidarity, he sought individual conversion, a voluntary solidarity, a fraternity founded on obedience to the will of Yahweh expressed in rational and humanitarian laws. This legislation completes the transition from primitive collectivism to individualism and to the interior religion that the prophets had proclaimed. Thus, the deuteronomic legislator also paved the way for the rise of the Jewish community.

The rise of Judaism

Causse argued that the formation of Judaism cannot be described simply in terms of a return from exile and restoration to Jerusalem; it was an evolution from an ethnic group to a religious community, which was from then on a diaspora. With the destruction of 586 BC, Israel became a people without land. Those left in Judah were of little significance; the centre of gravity and the vital forces of Judaism now lay in the diaspora. This diaspora included not just the Babylonian exiles, but also groups in Egypt and elsewhere deriving for the most part from before the destruction of Jerusalem. Without reference to Weber, Causse (*ibid.*, 187) describes this Israel as a pariah people, inhabiting the cities of others. Traditional institutions were no longer maintained; people were united now as much by community of interests and works, into guilds, as for the preservation of tradition. Only the family remained as a relatively stable organization, but in modified form: the role of the father declined while the influence of the mother increased; the family functioned for the preservation of the race and its moral education. The Jerusalem sanctuary was in ruins, but the word of the prophets and of the torah remained, and through these the communities of the diaspora affirmed themselves before the nations as a religious tradition rather than as a race.

The old conception of the solidarity of the group was now abandoned, but the vision of Israel as a single whole did not disappear. It remained as a hope or as a programme, though more and more detached from the present reality and linked with an apocalyptic future. The vision was a utopian programme projected into the future, as in Ezekiel 40 – 48, or set in Israel's past history, as in P. The covenant between God and Israel has here lost its primitive mysticism and notion of communion, and has become a judicial contract fixed in detail; it produces not a just society, as in Deuteronomy, but a church with its ritual. The society of Israelite clans and families has become a holy congregation, and its aim is less to maintain and renew the covenant with God as to ensure its purification through expiation and atonement. There is a rigid distinction between sacred and profane, but the ethical aspect of holiness, founded on individual repentance, is absent, and is replaced by a purely magical conception of purity and impurity. This is a programme, however, which did not suit the actual post-exilic situation in which the high priest had temporal as well as spiritual duties; centralization of the purified community around a single sanctuary could have only a theoretical significance for the majority of the diaspora. For the latter, it is through the torah that the individual, without the intermediation of the community, can lead a holy and perfect life.

Judaism in the sixth and fifth centuries was characterized by the formation of sects, voluntary religious organizations, without ethnic or political conditions, in which membership was not by right of birth or ancestry but through personal adherence to moral and ethical teaching. Sects had functioned in a limited way also in pre-exilic times: they were the contexts within which reform movements had developed. Their role in the diaspora, however, was much more significant, given the absence of a national framework and the disappearance of the ancient social groups. These sects in Babylon, Egypt and in Judah, collected and interpreted prophetic oracles, and collections of torah; they reinterpreted the psalms especially, as prayers of the pious afflicted ones, and cast themselves in the role of the poor oppressed by the wicked. Their fraternity was a spiritual one, based on ethical relationships rather than the old bond of consanguinity. The cult, whose ritual had formerly been the means by which the primitive group realized its unity, now had the purpose of leading the individual soul nearer to God. The consciousness of the individual worshipper is no longer lost in the collective, but affirms itself in the development of a personal piety. This development of a mystical piety was, however, exceptional; what was more characteristic of Judaism was faithfulness to the religious tradition and zeal for the torah. The teaching and explanation of the law separated the pure from the impure, and bound together faithful individuals in the same moral discipline and the same devotion.

The Jewish sect did not remain rigorously closed. Jewish literature of the time reflects a universalism and a missionary spirit in the diaspora communities. The religion of the law preserved Judaism, but it did not create an unbridgeable gulf between Judaism and the world since certain basic commandments, those of the covenant with Noah (Gen.9:1–7), embrace all of humanity. The universalistic tendencies of Judaism come to full expression in the wisdom literature of the fifth and fourth centuries. It makes no reference to Israel and its sacred tradition, but considers man simply as an individual, advocating a practical, reasonable morality which transcends sectarian and ethnic barriers. This universalistic tendency in Judaism, however, which emerged as the religious community organized itself on an individualistic basis outside the framework of political institutions, developed to only a very limited extent. With the accommodation of wisdom to the orthodox Jewish tradition, wisdom came to be identified with the torah. Judaism remained attached to a particular historical past: Yahweh was the God who had brought his people out of Egypt.

Causse was heavily influenced by the sociological tradition represented by Fustel de Coulanges, Robertson Smith and Durkheim. Here is rooted his understanding of the family as a cultic community, the gradual emergence of individualism out of a primitive collectivism, the basically ritualistic nature of primitive religion and the expression of social unity in primitive ritual. Into this sociological framework he then fitted that evolutionary theory on the significance of the prophets as those who introduced morality into religion, which may be traced to Reuss, Graf and Wellhausen.[2] The other major influence on Causse, however, and the one which is responsible for probably the major weakness in his work, is Lévy-Bruhl, for it was on the basis of the latter's early writings (cf. Kimbrough:1978,114ff.) that Causse tried to penetrate the mentality of primitive and civilized communities, in order to uncover the inner development of the transition from primitive collectivism to individualism. His adherence to the categories of pre-logical and logical thinking, which allowed him to state a development from a primitive collectivism binding together worshippers and their God into a ritual community, to an individual rationalism, went beyond what Durkheim considered the proper task of sociology. Moreover, it reflected an understanding of the nature of human thinking which was quickly shown to be inappropriate, at least for ancient Israel.[3]

The structural-functionalist tradition in later Old Testament study

Introduction
That sociological tradition which can be identified as rooted in Durkheim and as appearing in the work of Causse, is the implicit or explicit framework within which much sociological study of ancient Israel is currently being carried out. Within the last few years such study has enjoyed a remarkable resurgence, particularly in some of its distinctive strands of thought. The approach is marked by certain identifying characteristics: there is a concern for describing Israelite society as a total integrated system, frequently through the use of sociological models; the religion of Israel is seen as part of Israel's ideational superstructure which is dependably related to her social and economic structure, and ultimately to her agricultural and environmental foundation; the role of the individual as a real and effective influence in history and society is considerably weakened, if indeed it survives at all, and, correspondingly, the

significance of Old Testament texts, which are the work of individuals or describe Israel's history in individualistic, biographical terms, is severely devalued; a reliable objective body of information for the understanding of the nature and history of Israel is sought in archaeology, the study of agricultural resources and patterns of climate, and the nature and distribution of general environmental resources.

The theoretical framework of this approach, which is strikingly positivistic in its presuppositions, is clearly the so-called pyramid of culture. This model, with due allowance for a degree of complicating interaction between the different levels of the pyramid, posits an understanding of man and society according to which the basic determinant is ecological; on that basis there rests the social and economic structure; at the apex of the pyramid, and dependent on the lower levels, there are to be found the ideas and beliefs of society, including its religious beliefs.

This approach is given theoretical expression by Long (1982,243ff.), whose criticisms of Weber, Malamat and Hanson in particular are from this perspective: they do not adequately analyse Israelite society and give too much prominence to ideational features. Social study, he argues, is empirical in its approach, and agnostic in religious matters (*ibid.*,244); sociological study should be directed towards society as a functioning system of social relationships, and be concerned with living conditions, food supply, economic roles. Religious beliefs are one expression, and perhaps not always the most important expression, of socio-economic and political realities. Long may be to some extent over-simplifying the issue by claiming that sociology and sociological approaches, described in these terms, are 'but a form of the crisis posed by nineteenth century historical enquiry' (*ibid.*,244), since historical enquiry of that period had a strong idealistic content which, in this version of sociological study, is conspicuously lacking; he has, nevertheless, expressed the theory behind a significant trend in recent sociological approaches to ancient Israel.

In the review of this trend in relation to Israelite society and religion the work of Gottwald has particular importance. It is the most sustained attempt to provide a total sociological understanding of pre-monarchic Israelite society and religion. The separation here of its discussion of Israelite society from its discussion of Israelite religion is partly for reasons of convenience; the work does, however, reflect certain methodological obscurities and inconsistencies which make such a division also appropriate.

Israelite society in the structural-functionalist tradition
1. The inclusion here of Gottwald's *The Tribes of Yahweh* might at first seem surprising, especially since its author (1980,624ff.) dismisses Durkheim as an idealist, and (*ibid.*,631ff.) espouses an apparently Marxist approach to understanding society and the relationship of religion to society. There are substantial reasons, however, for putting Gottwald with Durkheim into the same sociological tradition.

First, the distinctive characteristics of conflict theory, which analyses society from the perspective of the interaction of different classes and status groups, are wholly absent from Gottwald's study; here, pre-monarchic Israel appears largely as a harmonious, undifferentiated unity.

Secondly, the reason for Gottwald's rejection of Durkheim as an idealist, that for Durkheim 'society emerges out of the group mind and objectifies itself symbolically in religion' (Gottwald:1980,625), could be held to reflect a rather one-sided reading of Durkheim. In Durkheim's thinking on the nature of society and the relationship of religion to society the real and the ideal are inseparable:

> In showing that religion is something essentially social, we do not mean to say that it confines itself to translating into another language the material forms of society and its immediate vital necessities. It is true that we take it as evident that social life depends upon its material foundation and bears its mark, just as the mental life of an individual depends upon his nervous system and in fact his whole organism. But collective consciousness is something more than a mere epiphenomenon of its morphological basis, just as individual consciousness is something more than a simple efflorescence of the nervous system (Durkheim:1976,423f.).

On the other hand, even if Durkheim's idealism is not to be overlooked, it cannot constitute a point of distinction between him and Gottwald, for the latter, despite his apparent espousal of historical materialism, has in fact provided an account of the origins of an egalitarian Israelite society which can only be described as idealist. This point will be developed further later.

Thirdly, Gottwald has adopted a functionalist approach to Israelite society and emphasized its synchronic, structural dimensions, rather than its diachronic and historical. His analysis of Israel can be seen as a reflection of Durkheim's approach which has been described as a 'holistic functionalism': it seeks to explain social facts by investigating the causes which produced them and the function they fulfil in promoting social solidarity (Swingewood:1984,227f.).

Fourthly, the form of Marxism which Gottwald has espoused, and on which he theorizes especially in connection with explaining the relationship of Israelite religion to Israelite society, is (as will be noted later) by no means typical of Marx as a founder of the conflict tradition. It is, rather, a version of Marxism useful to Gottwald's purpose of expounding the materialistic basis of religion; otherwise, religion is understood by him in structural-functionalist terms. The distinctive Marxist understanding of religion as ideology, which originated with class division in society and will disappear with the realization of the classless utopia, has no place in Gottwald's presentation. Gottwald's Marxism is a 'naturalistic Marxism' (Giddens: 1977,52ff.) which is quite compatible with the Durkheim tradition of sociology. The place of Marx as a conflict theorist has little significance in Gottwald's theoretical discussion of religion and society in Israel.

The Tribes of Yahweh has been described as 'a book that promises to become a classic'.[4] Although subtitled 'A Sociology of the Religion of Liberated Israel, 1250–1050 B.C.E.', the work is by no means concerned solely with the religion of Israel; rather, it analyses the nature of Israelite society as that to which its religion is dependably related, and within which it performs a particular function. The work is divided into two parts: the first is concerned with basic literary and historical questions, and culminates in a full and comprehensive analysis of the social structure of pre-monarchic Israel;[5] the second compares Israelite with non-Israelite social structures, and culminates in a discussion of the religion of Israel and its relationship to its social context.

In the first part, the literary discussion assembles the fragmentary sources which are held to derive from and reflect the life of pre-monarchic Israel. In the pre-monarchic cult there took place the process of tradition formation and the production of the national history in the Pentateuch, as 'the close literary counterpart of the sociocultural process of compromise and sublimation by which Israel became a sum greater than any of its segments' (Gottwald:1980,82). That is to say, as pre-monarchic Israel gradually forged its sociocultural identity as a totality comprehending yet transcending its various elements, so, in the cult, there emerged in a parallel process its national history, an account comprehending and also transcending the various traditional elements which it has taken up. The Israel to which this national history relates is pre-monarchic Israel; monarchic Israel could not be the context of formation of this history, because the monarchy was not a national institution expressive of the unity of Israel. The monarchy in fact brought to an end the national unity of Israel by introducing a divisive institution; the monarchy could not produce a national epic, but only such monarchic stories as the court history.

Gottwald's historical discussion deals only with the question of the origins of Israel. This is significant: his concern is not with the history of Israel in the period of the judges, but with the origins of an Israel which then simply existed in the period of the judges. The focus is not on the history of Israel but on the nature of Israel. Three different models have been used in reconstructing Israel's origins: conquest, immigration and revolt. The first is the biblical presentation which, in weaker or stronger form, is still widely adopted. The second has definite associations with the biblical presentation, in that it considers Israel to derive from outside the land; but it has fitted that presentation into a postulated socio-historical context which presumes that Israel's ancestors were semi-nomads whose form of life involved regular periods of residence within the settled agricultural area. The revolt model also postulates a socio-historical context: Canaan was a stress-torn feudalized society into which the exodus Israelites introduced a faith celebrating the centrality of deliverance from socio-political bondage. To this faith the oppressed Canaanite lower classes converted and, together with the exodus Israelites, proceeded to throw off the yoke of centralized political rule by imperial feudal kings. The direct biblical evidence for this revolt model is fairly slight, and before coming to a decision in its favour Gottwald turns to a discussion of the Israelite social system. The reason for this is that social structure and historical process go hand in hand, the one being reflected in the other; as the product of history, Israel's social structure should reveal what that history was.

Israelite society was tribal. The tribe was a territorial entity; it was based not on kinship, but first of all on territorial contiguity reinforced by other forms of association. Moreover, the tribe was a developed social form and cannot be considered a primary unit; it comprised smaller associations which are prior to it, the *mishpahah* or 'clan', and the *beth ab* or 'father's house'. The latter, comprising the family head, his wife, sons, unmarried daughters and sons' wives and grandchildren, was 'the basic economic unit in the Israelite social system. It formed a self-sufficient unit in the sense that it produced the basic means of subsistence for all its members and consumed all, or nearly all, of what it produced' (Gottwald, *ibid.*,292). The clan was a protective association of a number of such families, within which they intermarried. Although the father's house, or family, was the primary social unit, this does not imply that all power resided at this level. In the course of time instruments of government were formed, such as the council of elders at the tribal level, so that there developed a complex process of interaction from the bottom up and from the top down. This ensured the uniform development of tribal society throughout Israel, and at the same time preserved its fundamental egalitarian, non-authoritarian character.

This social form is often seen by anthropology as a secondary phenomenon, which arises in reaction to the pressure of more highly organized and dominant civilizations, as an organizational form imposed by those dominant civilizations in order to try to control and administer the subordinate elements. In Israel, however, tribalism was a consciously chosen social form, adopted as a radical alternative to the social structures of the environment.

Israel's tribalism was an autonomous project which tried to roll back the zone of political centralization in Canaan, to claim territory and peoples for an egalitarian mode of agricultural and pastoral life . . . All the evidence for early Israel points to its tribalism as a self-constructed instrument of resistance and of decentralized self-rule rather than tribalism as an administrative structure imposed by Canaanite rulers in order to govern proto-Israelite or Israelite subjects . . . Israel's tribalism was politically conscious and deliberate social revolution, and, more loosely, a civil war in that it divided and counterposed peoples who had previously been organized within Canaanite city states (*ibid.*,325).

Gottwald confirms his presentation by a discussion of Canaanite society in the context of which Israelite tribalism emerged. Feudalized Canaan was in a state of anarchy, each city state ruler attempting to expand his power at the expense of the others. Their protestations of loyalty in letters to the Egyptian Pharaoh accuse their rivals of being *habiru*, a loose and pejorative application of a term which primarily refers to outlaws who, to escape taxation, corvée, slavery, have withdrawn from society and subsist as armed mercenaries.

The wider social framework within which this unrest belonged was characterized by a division between the ruling urban élite and the subject peasantry. The normal distinction drawn between the settled and the nomadic or semi-nomadic way of life is rejected by Gottwald. Pure nomadism is irrelevant to this context; semi-nomadism, which is relevant, was, however, an offshoot of the settled way of life and cannot be sharply distinguished from the agricultural mode of existence: 'agriculture and pastoral nomadism are by no means mutually exclusive but are often combined in the same human community in manifold forms. The full implications of this undoubted socioeconomic fact have yet to be applied historically and sociologically to pastoral nomadism in the environment of early Israel' (*ibid.*,439). Semi-nomadism, or pastoralism, is a marginal development, a specialized offshoot of the agricultural-pastoral village community, with which it belongs as one socio-economic way of life over against urbanism.

The socio-economic category to which early Israel belongs is clear: it is the agricultural-pastoral sector. This has important implications when used as the framework for understanding the patriarchs and Israelite origins: the patriarchs are not cultural foreigners in the land; Israelites have a strong indigenous rootage in the land. Early Israel's achievement consisted in this, that it brought together the diverse underclasses in the land which the feudal system had until then controlled and divided: the *habiru*, pastoralists and depressed peasantry. Israel's vehement and tenacious identity as a single people had its basis and focus in an anti-feudal egalitarian social commitment. The existence of Israel is not to be explained solely in terms of a people delivered from Egypt in the exodus. Before that group arrived there was an Israel already in the land, an Israel characterized by militarization (the *habiru*), by decentralized socio-political co-operation on the part of a tribal society which excluded hierarchic leadership or formal unity, and by a common cult centred on the worship of El. The exodus group contributed to this situation a growth in numbers, revolutionary zeal which acted as a catalyst among underclass Canaanites, and the common cult of Yahweh. The opponents of Israel were not Canaanites as such, but the city state rulers and royal bastions. Israel's uniqueness is to be described in socio-political terms: this was the only example in the ancient Near East of the underclasses in a feudal society overthrowing their lords and setting up an egalitarian social system.

2. Gottwald's major study of pre-monarchic Israel has become the focus of continuing discussion. Two critical responses of some significance which may be considered here are those of Lenski (1980) and Brandfon (1981).[6]

Lenski, while agreeing that Israelite origins lie in social revolution, has argued that this should not be seen as a unique process, but rather should be set alongside the emergence of those societies which developed as counter-cultures in marginal or frontier territories, as in the United States of America, Australia and South Africa. The leaders of agrarian societies in the past often found it difficult to maintain effective control over those areas which were remote from urban centres or located in mountainous regions. The counter-cultures that tended to develop in such areas shared many of the social and cultural patterns which Gottwald attributes to early Israel: they were antagonistic to the traditional centres of power; they developed populist and democratic ideologies, often of a religious nature; they tended to live in small farms, but as they grew and prospered they also tended to revert to some extent to the more traditional ways of life.

This modification of Gottwald's presentation is perhaps more fundamental than might at first appear. It suggests that Israel's origins should be set within the framework of Canaanite expansionist activity in opening up the highlands, a view which has, in general, found considerable favour as in some of the works to be noted below. For the moment, however, it should be remarked that it also presupposes that the phenomenon of pre-monarchic tribal Israel was by nature a transitory phenomenon which must inevitably develop along the lines of the social structure of that society at the frontier of which it originated. This aspect has been noted by Chaney (1983,48ff.), who has accepted the frontier model as a healthy corrective to the idea of social revolt. This revolt involved not just the ideological rejection of, and withdrawal from, the political structures of the time, but the geographical and physical separation of people from the city state areas of Palestine into the marginal territories on the mountains. Such movements and the societies resulting from them were usually temporary, and were gradually overtaken by the traditional system.

Gottwald (1983[a]) has in turn questioned this proposal, in the belief that the frontier model has only limited reference to Israel and should be subordinated to the social revolt model. It is derived from social contexts (such as the American conquest of the West) which are inappropriate to the situation of Israel since they presuppose the frontier as a frontier of capitalist and imperialist expansion and domination. In addition, however, it is clearly also the case that Gottwald is unwilling to compromise the independence of the Israelite phenomenon as a unique revolutionary experiment, the development of which was 'aborted' (Gottwald:1980,33) by the introduction of the monarchy into Israel.

The discussion of the most appropriate model by which to understand Israel's origins is an important one, and still continues. No less important is a more philosophical issue noted by Brandfon, which points to a problem if not indeed a certain incoherence fundamental to Gottwald's whole presentation. In his discussion of the relationship between religion and society, Gottwald has thoroughly criticized and rejected any hint of idealism, claiming that historical materialism offers the only coherent and sociologically satisfactory strategy. Moreover, his outline of the course which, in his view, future research into Israelite history and society should take (1980,650ff.) has a materialist basis: it should be concerned with investigating the forces and relations of production, economic geography, population growth and distribution, the cultural and social context of archaeological finds, the technological base formed by iron, water cisterns and irrigation, rock terraces, and its effect on the growth of Israel. This is clearly a thoroughly materialistic programme.

On the other hand, however, Gottwald's actual presentation of the origins of Israel does not reflect this kind of programme, but rather comes very close to the idealist position which Bright represents and which Gottwald rejects so emphatically: his reconstruction presupposes that the people of Canaan intellectually understood their economic plight and devised an ideal scheme as an alternative; the peasants' revolt was then an idea which gradually won over the oppressed peasant class. Marxism here plays the role that in other reconstructions, such as that of Mendenhall, is played by Yahwism.

This becomes particularly clear in Gottwald's account (1980,493ff.) of the contribution of the exodus Yahwists to the rise of the tribal society of Israel. Before the arrival of the exodus group, there was an Israel already present in Palestine, comprising 'segmentary social units, of a broadly "band-like" or "tribal" character, clustered together in a community of perceived interests that facilitated coordinated actions while excluding hierarchic leadership or formal unity' (*ibid.*,495). These social units had a common cult, the worship of El, a common name, Israel, and were characterized by a tradition of military capability. To this Israel the exodus Yahwists contributed, firstly, 'an increase in the number, socioeconomic types, and previous historical experiences of the groups entering the community' (*ibid.*,496), secondly, a revolutionary zeal forged in the experience of freedom from Egypt, which energized and guided the existing coalition of underclass Canaanites, and, thirdly, the common cult of Yahweh which, more than the cult of the Canaanite high god El, could symbolize the anti-imperial and anti-feudal ideology of the diffuse egalitarian community. It is quite clearly impossible to fit this account into the type of materialistic framework which Gottwald thinks appropriate, and, indeed, in so far as Gottwald stresses that Yahwistic Israel comprised a 'socioeconomically variegated . . . association of peoples' (*ibid.*,497), there is little in the theoretical foundation of this presentation to distinguish him from Weber. Revolutionary Yahwistic Israel came into being on the basis of an egalitarian idea, coming to symbolic expression as Yahwism, which overcame the socio-economic, historical and geographical diversity of its constituent elements.

3. A point made by Brandfon (1981,108f.) is that Gottwald ignores the possibility that social egalitarianism in Canaan may have been an unintended consequence of a variety of events in the Late Bronze Age. That social phenomena are, in part at least, the unintended consequences of a variety of events, is a major plank in the materialist platform, for it helps to validate the view that men are the product of their environment and cannot be understood as the determinative influence on history and society. This view has two important and related consequences. On the one hand, it leads to a devaluation of reconstructions of Israelite history, society and religion which are based on the text of the Old Testament, because the Old Testament presupposes that men (and God) do make history. On the other hand, it encourages the attribution of a much more dominating role in historical reconstruction to non-biblical resources; these either allow a better understanding of Israel's environment, which is seen as the foundation of the social structures that Israel adopted, or provide sociological models within the framework of which Israel as a total society might be understood.

The first of these consequences is reflected in Whitelam's critique (1986) of current attempts to write the history of Israel, and his advocacy of the priority of archaeology. Current history writing is concerned with the unique event or individual, and is exclusively dependent on written sources. The problem with this is that these written sources are not history; they are literary creations which at best reflect the particular perception of the history held by the authors. Such texts cannot be regarded as primary historical sources. Moreover, the concentration of current history writing on unique events and great individuals reflects the belief that great men dictate the course of history. This view, which simply perpetuates the bias of the written sources themselves, must be given up in favour of a systematic consideration of the role and inter-relationship of all social groups in all periods. History's concern should be with the study of the recurrent and the regular, not with the unique, in terms of either events or individuals; it should aim to develop long term perspectives and show patterns of change over long periods of time.

The second consequence of the materialist approach, a reliance for historical understanding on non-biblical sources, is reflected in those studies which emphasize the contribution of archaeology and those which make use of sociological models consciously adopted from elsewhere and applied to the Israelite context. These concerns are, of course, not incompatible, and are often found together: the archaeologist is understood to supply the objectively reliable data which may be set within the framework of the chosen sociological model.

The 'new archaeology' is particularly conscious of its role in this different, non-biographical, approach to history (see Whitelam:1986,45ff.; de Geus:1982,50ff.). It concentrates not on the study of particular sites in isolation, but on more general surveys which reveal patterns of settlement and the relationship between sites. Its concern is with the social and cultural context of archaeological data, with subsistence agriculture and pastoralism, and with seeing how archaeological remains may reflect ideological aspects of a society. This archaeology has undermined the historian's traditional reliance on written records (Whitelam:1986,58), and has indeed in some instances shown the mythical character of those records. So, against the biblical presentation of Israelite origins, it has shown the essential continuity of culture during the transition between the Late Bronze Age and the early Iron Age. The main question which it throws up is that of the relationship between the decline and destruction of Palestinian urban centres and the growth of dispersed rural settlements. This is to be interpreted as a move away from the centres of urban control, following the decline of the material prosperity and political effectiveness of the urban centres. Thus, the growth of the highland settlements is the result, not the cause, of urban economic collapse. As the dispersed rural settlements expanded and multiplied, there emerged competition for available land; it is this which led to the formation of the state, so that the monarchy must then be considered to be the result of internal pressures, as well as of external social and environmental constraints (see also Chaney:1986,53ff.).

The information yielded by archaeology and the study of Israel's environment is usually fragmentary and incomplete. The current popular appeal to models derived from outside the Israelite context is an attempt to compensate for this lack and to provide, even though these are simply models and as such idealist constructions even in their original contexts, objective knowledge about the nature of Israel.

It has now become common to think of pre-monarchic Israel as a segmentary society. This is a term used of Israel already by Durkheim (1933,177); more recently it has been argued by Crüsemann (1978,201ff.) and Schäfer-Lichtenberger (1983,333ff.), using the work of Sigrist, and Fortes and Evans-Pritchard, that pre-monarchic Israel was a genealogically ordered segmentary society comprising equal unilinear descent groups.[7] The analogy is not without its difficulties, however. There is considerable dispute about the very nature of a segmentary society: most descriptions go back to the study of the Nuer by Fortes and Evans-Pritchard, but significant aspects of this are now questioned (Fiensy:1987,73ff.). Moreover, what are understood to be essential marks of a segmentary society, such as the absence of primogeniture and of parental authority, and legal power exercised within small groups (Rogerson:1986,20ff.), are not to be found in Israel.

Segmentary division is in fact characteristic of societies which do not follow the egalitarian pattern normally attributed to this type, and is found particularly in ranked societies or chiefdoms (Lemche:1985,219ff.). The chiefdom also has been considered as a suitable model for Israel, either under Saul and during the early part of David's reign (Flanagan:1981,47ff.), or even, as an association of chiefdoms, through the period of the judges (Rogerson:1986,22ff.). The chiefdom differed from the egalitarian segmentary society in that the ranking of its lineages promoted centralization and retarded the divisive tendencies present with equal lineage systems.

The introduction of sociological models provides a framework not only for understanding the general course of Israelite social development, but also for attaining a more precise exegesis of biblical texts. In Bellefontaine's discussion (1987) of the judicial background presupposed by 2 Samuel 14:4–21, it is proposed that David's rule should be understood as that of a chieftain rather than that of a king; it belongs, therefore, within a period of transition in the development of Israel from an acephalous, segmentary society to a state. In the former, law is customary law, administered by the local community, oral in form and applied by a judge who is not a professional jurist. In the latter (as reflected in Jehoshaphat's judicial reform, recorded in 2 Chronicles 19), the centralized power of the state takes most judicial power away from the local communities and concentrates it, as part of the centralizing tendency of the state system, in the hands of the king. A chieftainship is characterized by a degree of centralization, with the chief as final court of appeal. Some judicial independence remains, however, at the local village level, and the chief is unable completely to subordinate the authority of regionally based power groups. Such a transitional stage is reflected in David's initial reluctance to intervene on behalf of the widow in her appeal against the judgment on her son legitimately reached by the local community. At her insistence, however, and without questioning the customary law which had been enacted by the community, David agreed to exert his chiefly judicial authority, so weakening the autonomy of the local community.

4. Characteristic of non-biographical accounts of Israel's history is the subordination of concern both with the effective actions of individuals and with unique events; such accounts are also marked by concentration on the system of Israelite society seen as a totality, and on her history as part of an overall pattern or long term trend, in which Israel is little more than an inevitable result of movements and developments over which she has no control. These two concerns, with the total community, on the one hand, and with long term developments, on the other, are by no means unrelated. Both are effects of the move away from history writing in its biographical form; the latter not only emphasizes the individual at the expense of the total society of which he is part, but it also tends towards a foreshortening of the past, which becomes concentrated in the life of the individual. With the move away from an approach centred on the individual and the unique event, history writing then takes on both a broad synchronic aspect and a much more long term perspective. At a later stage some criticism of the presuppositions involved here will be expressed; for the present, however, it is important to clarify their effects on the reconstruction of Israelite history, and indeed also to emphasize the significant·contribution which this approach to the subject has made.

The attempt to bring together the synchronic understanding of Israel and the long term diachronic perspective on her history represents a significant advance over the rather static presentations that sociological studies in the structural-functionalist tradition often take. Two such attempts are particularly noteworthy:[8] the first, by Frick (1985), is concentrated on the immediate context of the development of the Israelite state; the other, by Coote and

Whitelam (1986;1987), takes a very long term perspective on the rise of Israel and the emergence of the Israelite state.

Frick's work puts the rise of the state in the context of comprehensive sociological theory. Having criticized the biographical approach to history as incapable of doing justice to the enormous complexity of interactions in even a simple social system, he reviews some general theories which describe history as an evolutionary process. Fried and Service are noted as being more concerned with elaborating a general taxonomy (band, tribe, chiefdom, state) than with classifying types of change and evolutionary transformation. Gall and Saxe think in terms of ecological succession, using taxonomy as a framework for assessing and explaining changes which take place in the relationships between the variables in a system as it develops. Adams proposes a growth sequence, arising from an internal dynamic in a system, which repeats itself in the course of human social evolution. If any such theoretical approaches are to be taken seriously, Frick argues, it is obviously impossible to explain the rise of the Israelite state solely by reference to the Philistines. Rather, the Philistines were only one of the dependent variables, a necessary but not a sufficient cause, in the rise of the state. They accelerated the emergence of the state from an existing chiefdom, the latter being the 'societal form that had already, as an adaptive strategy, necessarily gone beyond any reputed early egalitarianism' (Frick:1985,26).

Frick argues for a synthetic approach which sees the state as the result of a number of factors without any single prime mover.[9] Such an approach is supplied by the model of cultural evolution; this provides for different evolutionary trajectories relating to variations in agricultural risk, diversity and productivity, as well as to the size and character of the environment. The evolutionary trajectories arising from the interaction of these factors are forms of development from an egalitarian society to a stratified society or chiefdom and then to a state.[10] In the Israelite context, it is only by analogy, rather than on the basis of direct evidence, that its original segmentary, egalitarian stage can be sketched. The chiefdom stage, however, can be reconstructed on the basis of both archaeology and the Old Testament text. The chiefdom develops out of the egalitarian segmentary society when the 'localized autonomies' which comprise the latter 'come to recognize the superior authority of one of their own in a grouping of small polities' (Frick,*ibid.*,77). The role of the chief is then strengthened by his filling of subordinate posts with kinsmen and on the basis of a body of clients built up with his wealth. Such socio-political change, Frick argues, is not determined by techno-environmental factors, but these do allow for a range of adaptations, some of which, for internal reasons in the societies concerned, are susceptible to the centralizing tendencies inherent in a chiefdom.

The development to a chiefdom in pre-monarchic Israel took place within the constraints of environmental variables of which two are most important: water and soil (Frick:1985,101ff.). As far as the first is concerned, an analysis of rainfall patterns in the central highlands shows that they constitute a medium risk agricultural environment. This means that for subsistence agriculture both water conservation techniques and also suitable socio-political strategies for their implementation would have to be developed. There is evidence for the development of agricultural terracing on the hillsides before the formation of the state. This is a labour intensive system designed to increase fertility and yield, which requires co-operation between families and villages and so inhibits fissioning in society. As far as soil as a determinant is concerned, analysis of soil types, according to four basic types ranging from potentially quite productive to relatively unproductive, shows different proportions of these in the central highlands. This analysis can be correlated with archaeological sites to show that sites are located on freely drained land with at least two, and sometimes more, soil types nearby. Thus, successful sites maximize agricultural diversity and spread risk by being able to exploit alternatives should one fail.

Tel Masos is taken by Frick (*ibid.*,159ff.) as a particular example of a site which shows evidence of the existence of a chiefdom: it is larger than others in the vicinity which, as indicated by pottery, were related to it; the site had one superior type of building; there is evidence of public works projects related to agricultural production, which indicates co-operation between groups and a degree of specialization of labour from administration through to actual food production. 'The mechanism that maintained social solidarity and law and order on the village and inter-village level and made possible multicommunity groupings in pre-state Israel may very well have been a unifying religious ideology and ritual not unlike that suggested by the amphictyonic model, but one which was much more flexible in its organization' (*ibid.*,165f.).

Thus, the development of Israel from a segmentary society to a chiefdom in the time of Saul and the early part of David's reign, to statehood under the later David and Solomon, represents a process of adaptive transformations in which the role of agriculture is of prime importance. Environmental uncertainties selected those technologies and social structures that could maximize the capabilities of the labour supply (*ibid.*, 197). When labour needs required a level of efficiency and specialization beyond that which could be supplied by the local household, then the chief and his clients emerged to organize and direct energy exchanges between the different segments of society. 'As labor became more specialized, this in turn could lead to the more sophisticated and compulsory controls of the state' (*ibid.*, 202).

The studies of Coote and Whitelam complement that of Frick by setting the origins of Israel and the rise of the Israelite state within the context of very long term processes of expansion and decline. The study of economic geography and long term settlement patterns is argued to be the foundation of any history which aims to transcend the short term perspectives of traditional political and biographical histories. Literary records, especially the biblical record, are rejected as unsuitable for this task since the use of them simply perpetuates the theological bias and particular interests of their authors (1987, 17ff.). The Pentateuch emphasizes the unity of Israel in the interests of legitimizing the unity of the Davidic empire. The real circumstances of Israel's emergence have been forgotten since they did not serve the purposes of the ruling élite and certainly not the Davidic need to emphasize the unity of Israel under his rule. By contrast, archaeological surface surveys allow the historian to build up a network of demographic, economic and political interrelationships, and by using these along with social science categories it will be possible to recreate the historical past despite the poverty of data. Moreover, a synthesis within an extended chronological perspective will free biblical studies from the merely descriptive or chronological histories which concentrate on what happened, to ask the more fundamental question of why it happened (*ibid.*, 22).

The emergence of Israel is to be seen in the long term framework of major phases of expansion and contraction of settlement within Palestine, and not in the context of supposed cultural change through invasion from outside. The Near East is marked by a cyclic pattern of decline and regeneration, which may be observed from the Early Bronze Age to the present. The expansion of settlement into the highlands of Canaan is sometimes (as in the case of the emergence of Israel) a shift away from the lowlands caused by urban decline resulting from the disruption of international trade, and the need to establish an alternative pastoral-agricultural economy; sometimes such expansion is the result of outside investment during a period of political stability conducive to increased trade. Israel first appeared during an imperial power vacuum associated with a drop in trade in the thirteenth century. The decline in trade, precipitated by the weakening or disappearance, for unknown reasons, of the Mycenaean and Hittite empires, Egyptian power and city states along the Levantine coast, affected not only urban élites but also peasants, pastoral nomads and bandits, all of whom were directly or indirectly linked to the wider economy. These groups, formerly subject to urban control to a greater or lesser degree, became increasingly independent. Their expansion of agriculture and pastoralism in the highlands was a means of risk reduction following the general economic collapse. The new sites established in the highlands cannot be understood to have originated as the result of conquest, infiltration or ideological conflict; otherwise the lack of fortifications in some of them and their location on the edge of the coastal plain are difficult to understand. Rather, they resulted from general withdrawal from the more exposed lowlands to other areas once urban decline had set in. The primary motivation behind them was a will to survive rather than specific ideological conviction. This was a development internal to Palestine, not one introduced from outside. The exploitation of the agricultural potentialities of the highlands through terracing and commercial tree cultivation required political stability, and Israel was the form in which that stability was achieved. Israel was thus the result not of conquest, nor of peasant revolt, but of economic change. Peasants, already involved in agriculture, nomads and bandits came together in the context of an economic crisis and developed agriculture as an alternative subsistence economy. Their reconciliation permitted increased food production, which in turn led to a rising population and an increase in highland settlements (Coote and Whitelam: 1987,27ff.,117ff.).

The gradual reestablishment of trade along with an upturn in the interregional economy led to the rise of the monarchy.

The Israelite monarchy came into existence, therefore, as part of that process to which the origins of Israel also belong. The monarchy is not to be seen as an alien institution forced on Israel by the Philistine threat. This, which is essentially the biblical picture, reflects the common tendency for societies and those in power to externalize crisis and social change. Rather, the Israelite monarchy was the result of numerous internal and external social and environmental forces, which are best understood by use of Carneiro's theory of circumscription (*ibid.*,146f.; see also Hauer:1986,3ff.). According to this theory, the state is the result of internal stimuli in response to social and environmental circumscription. Within a limited geographical area, further confined by Philistine imperialism and a network of lowland city states, the environment became 'impacted': a developing population exerted increasing pressure on limited resources, leading to agricultural intensification and political centralization. The rise of the monarchy was then a part of a process which goes back to the birth of Israel, in which a reversal of the factors that led to her emergence set in immediately: the economic decline became an expanding economy; diminished socio-economic stratification became increasing stratification; decentralization gave way to interest in eventual centralization, as an emergent landed class attempted to preserve the power and privileged position which their increasing wealth had created for them. The monarchy was the means by which a subgroup of emergent landed élite in Israel imposed greater costs of national defence on village smallholders and retained political control over participation in trade among themselves.

Israelite religion and society in the structural-functionalist tradition
1. Durkheim's understanding of religion as a social fact, a system of beliefs and practices which functioned to bind society together, has been highly influential. Perhaps his most ardent disciple was Swanson (1964), who attempted to provide empirical confirmation for Durkheim's view by correlating major varieties in religious belief with analogous variations in social structure. For Swanson, the supernatural was experienced in social life because social relationships have inherent supernatural qualities; they are at the same time immanent, in that they are realized in particular experiences, and transcendent, in that they continuously influence experience in general. So the form taken

The Old Testament in Sociological Perspective

by social relationships must be reflected in the form which religious conceptions take and correlations can be established between them. Swanson's programme is an ambitious one; he was unable, however, to relate immediate social experience to the macro-structures which he took as determinative of religious forms, nor could he adequately explain the exceptions to the correlations which he established. Moreover, as Bowker (1973,29) noted, what he analysed was not the origin of the sense of God (which is what Durkheim claimed to have done), but the ways in which some senses of God, which may well be derived initially from other resources of meaning, were expressed and clothed imaginatively.

2. The structural-functionalist understanding of the relationship of religion to society has been applied most consistently and thoroughly to ancient Israel by Gottwald (1980,608ff.). In his view, religion is a function of society, that is, it stands in a relationship of dependence on society. So, Yahwism is a function of Israelite society, and specifically of socio-political egalitarianism in pre-monarchic Israel. Mono-Yahwism, 'the innovative, non-philosophical, practical monotheism of early Israel', was 'the function of sociopolitical egalitarianism in premonarchic Israel' (*ibid.*,611). Two statements go some way towards providing a general explanation and justification for this claim:

This functional proposition means that mono-Yahwism is viewed as dependably related to sociopolitical egalitarianism in the sense that any strengthening or weakening or alteration in Israel's sociopolitical egalitarianism enhanced the probability of a strengthening, weakening, or alteration in Israelite mono-Yahwism (*ibid.*,611f.).

The dependable relatedness of mono-Yahwism to sociopolitical egalitarianism, stated positively, means that the fundamental intention of Israel to limit the exercise of power by any one person or group within the intertribal system, in order to ensure egalitarianism . . . *enhanced the probability* that the community would adopt or, as necessary, create a religion that did not usurp communal resources or communal power but rather legitimated the egalitarian impulse. The same functional dependence, stated negatively, means that had Israel been unconcerned with economic egalitarianism and the diffusion of communal power roles, i.e., had it developed social stratification and kingship or oligarchy at its inception, *the probability is enhanced* that it would have adopted a religion that was politically dominating and whose cult made large claims upon communal resources (*ibid.*,617).

The social egalitarian relations of Israelites provided the initiating motive and the energy in bringing the Yahwist religious innovation into being. The relationship between society and religion was not, however, a matter of one way traffic, for the Yahwist religion in turn acted back upon society in order to sustain the foundational egalitarian social relations. So one must allow for

the reciprocal and reinforcing impact of Yahwism on the primary social relations rooted in production. Ample room is present for semi-independent religious initiatives . . . on the model of fundamental initiative lying in the social relations from which the variously elaborated religious developments 'feed back' toward the strengthening or the weakening, the maintaining or the altering, of the given stream of social relations (*ibid.*,643).

In fact, the Yahwistic cult and ideology validated and motivated egalitarian social relations to so great an extent that it proved to be what Gottwald (*ibid.*,646) calls 'the single most significant servomechanism for the society'. By this he means that Yahwism, as a symbolic objectification of egalitarian social relations, worked back upon society in such a way that it strengthened those relations and inhibited any developments which might have undermined that unique social structure. To that extent, then, one can speak of Israelite society being a function of Yahwism, that is, that the Israelite egalitarian social system was dependably related to Yahweh as sole God of Israel, who motivated and sustained the desired system of social relations.

Gottwald's approach thus far is structural-functionalist, but it is an approach which he himself regards as in the end unsatisfactory. This is so, not because such a corresponding relationship between religion and society is open to question, but because it is essentially non-historical and atemporal, in that it is concerned with the interlocking and mutually supporting influence of religion and society at a given moment only.

107

Societies, however, do change, and functionalism, in Gottwald's view, is inadequate in so far as it provides no method for determining how such change takes place; in the end, functional models fail to be explanatory of social phenomena, and, since religion is a social phenomenon, structural-functionalism can provide no explanation of religion (*ibid.*,610f.,622ff.).[11]

Weber's analysis of the relationship between religion and society is, in Gottwald's rather one-sided interpretation of it, no more explanatory than structural-functionalism.

> In Weber's approach, this notion [viz., Weber's supposedly idealistic understanding of charisma] of 'asocial' or 'supersocial' sources of religion operates both at the beginning and throughout the course of historic religions. For ancient Israel it would apply equally to the origins of Yahwism with Moses and the redirection of Yahwism by the prophets. The 'founders' or 'reformers' of religion retain their inner mystery; it is only after they have launched their beliefs into the social stream that we can begin to trace causes and effects, selective adaptations and selective sloughings-off of this or that aspect of religion . . . Thus there remains in Weber's outlook the idealist 'escape hatch' of the great personalities as the mysterious sources of religions which are later adapted into a social routine. In such a formulation of the religion – society nexus there is no way of penetrating to the social matrix in which the religious innovators themselves are formed . . . An artificial division results between a pure presocial religion of epic personalities and a mixed, diluted, selected social religion suitable to the interests of classes and status groups. To my mind, however, we must come to terms with Moses and the prophets, as with all religious innovators, as propagandists for a religion already formed or forming in a given social field, and thus from the start a thoroughly mixed, diluted, and selected religion (*ibid.*,630).

In the end, Gottwald turns to Marxist historical materialism in order to supplement the structural-functionalist approach and so reach a total explanation of the relationship of religion to society. The view is ascribed to Marx that 'at the root of all social organization and mental ideation, including religion, is the way human beings within nature act upon nature to produce their means of subsistence and thereby fashion their own social nature' (*ibid.*,631), and this is accepted as being 'the most coherent and promising understanding for developing research strategies in the social sciences. It provides a framework within which to include structural-functional models as stepping stones in the analytic task of determining how social evolution occurs' (*ibid.*,633). So Marx is quoted with approval:

> We do not set out from what men say, imagine, conceive, nor from men as narrated, thought of, imagined, conceived, in order to arrive at men in the flesh. We set out from real active men, and on the basis of their real life-process we demonstrate the development of the ideological reflexes and echoes of this life process . . . Morality, religion, metaphysics, all the rest of ideology and their corresponding forms of consciousness, thus no longer retain the semblance of independence. They have no history, no development; but men, developing their material production and their material intercourse, alter, along with this their real existence, their thinking and the products of their thinking. Life is not determined by consciousness, but consciousness by life. In the first method of approach the starting point is consciousness taken as the living individual; in the second method, which conforms to real life, it is the real living individuals themselves, and consciousness is considered solely as *their* consciousness (*ibid.*,633).

In Gottwald's view, this means that 'changes in the forms of production (including techniques and modes of cooperative labor) lead correlatively to changes in social and political forms and to changes in ideas, including religious ideas' (*ibid.*,634). Modes of production do change with developing technology; these bring about new forms of social interaction, and these in turn lead to changes in ideas. Religious ideas then function to reflect and provide a mystical validation for the social order.

In a qualification of this presentation, Gottwald holds that

> it is not the mere givenness of society that projects a god image of the Yahweh type, but it is the tensions within the onward-moving social process, the breaks and leaps, the struggles and mutations in the 'distancing' process that occurs when a new social formation comes into being and people are 'stretched' to realize new possibilites of social interaction (*ibid.*,697f.).

Those who are ' "stretched" to realize new possibilities' are not, of course, charismatic innovators; rather, they are the victims of the 'tensions within the onward-moving social process'. As changes occur in the economic base, so tensions arise in the process of formation of new social structures, and then new ideas emerge as the deposit and reflection of these changes and developments.

In this way the religion of Israel first emerged.

'Yahweh' is the historically concretized, primordial power to establish and sustain social equality in the face of counter-oppression from without and against . . . nonegalitarian tendencies from within the society. 'The Chosen People' is the distinctive self-consciousness of a society of equals created in the intertribal order and demarcated from a primarily centralized and stratified surrounding world. 'Covenant' is the bonding of decentralized social groups in a larger society of equals committed to cooperation without authoritarian leadership and a way of symbolizing the locus of sovereignty in such a society of equals. 'Eschatology', or hope for the future, is the sustained commitment of fellow tribesmen to a society of equals with the confidence and determination that this way of life can prevail against great environmental odds (*ibid.*,692).

Religion is a function of social relations, and so forms of theology which have lost their relationship to religion understood in this way are 'independent intellectual games' (*ibid.*,703). Theological developments of this kind took place in Israel during the monarchic period: Israel became a statist society like many others in the ancient Near East, and so lost touch with her religion which proclaimed her to be unique. The social and economic truth behind the doctrine of the election of Israel, which is the uniqueness of Israel in welding together 'an autonomous egalitarian social, economic, and political life out of heterogeneous struggling groups', disappeared with the rise of the monarchy. It was then that the Old Testament doctrine of the election of Israel emerged as the 'objectification and reification of an actual reality into such a form and context that it becomes an embalmed relic and grotesque parody of the original truth' (*ibid.*,702).

110

3. It has already been noted that there is a serious fundamental discontinuity and lack of consistency in Gottwald's treatment: the philosophical presuppositions of his account of the rise of pre-monarchic Israel are in the end idealist; on the other hand, his explicit account of the relationship between religion and society (and, indeed, his programme for future research into Israelite society) are materialist. This is a serious discrepancy since it means that, on the one hand, he views Israelite society as based upon the ideas and understandings of its founders, who were creating an alternative society to the statist systems of their environment, while, on the other hand, he argues that these same ideas and understandings are the product of that alternative, egalitarian Israelite society.

Although Gottwald claims Marx as the foundation of his materialist view, it is rather his idealist account of the origins of Israelite society which is closer to Marx.[12] In Marx's view, it is not nature or technology which creates human society; it is man himself who does so in terms of his already existing ideas and values. These ideas and values indeed have a materialist origin in the real conditions of human life, but they are the product of history and of man's ongoing encounter with his environment. Consciousness is a social product, which originates in the interaction of men together in history and in their dealings with nature; consciousness is that through which men apprehend the world and in terms of which men change it. When Marx argued that 'life is not determined by consciousness but consciousness by life', he did not imply that consciousness is a mere epiphenomenon of the environment; rather, against the Hegelian view that men's ideas come from a supernatural, mysterious source, Marx was arguing that consciousness is the product of the history of men evolving in material circumstances. Men do make history, and they do so in terms of their consciousness. A Marxist view of Israelite origins would, therefore, hold that on the basis of ideas forged in the conflict situation of the class societies in the Canaanite city states, groups of disaffected created an alternative egalitarian society.

If this is so, then the Yahwistic faith of this Israel cannot be seen as the function of Israelite society in the materialist terms which Gottwald uses. If a correlation between Israelite faith and society exists, then it will rather take the form that Israel's religious ideas, forged and developing in her ongoing historical

111

experience, are the basis to her society. Gottwald's attempt to justify the reverse order of priority in fact depends more on the anthropological theory of Marvin Harris, to whom he explicitly appeals, than it does on Marx. Harris argued that human institutions and ideas are the direct results of natural circumstances: so, the cow is a sacred animal in India, not for theological reasons, but for its economic value. This is an explicitly determinist view of human consciousness, which is much closer to the mechanistic materialism of Feuerbach, which Marx criticized precisely on the grounds that it failed to recognize the role of human consciousness, than it is to Marx. 'The chief defect of all hitherto existing materialism (that of Feuerbach included) is that the thing, reality, sensuousness, is conceived only in the form of the object or of contemplation, but not as sensuous human activity, practice, not subjectively' (Marx:1977,156).

It is true that Marx gave some reason for the claim of a crude materialism to the designation Marxist. So, he argued (*ibid.*,164): 'The production of ideas, of conceptions, of consciousness, is at first directly interwoven with the material activity and the material intercourse of men, the language of real life. Conceiving, thinking, the mental intercourse of men, appear at this stage as the direct efflux of their material behaviour.' Marx wrote in these terms, however, within the context of a theoretical evolutionary scheme which posited a pre-class stage of society characterized by lack of differentiation and by common ownership of property, in which consciousness was the direct reflection of social and economic circumstances (cf.Giddens:1971,208); it was with the development of the family, private property and the state, that class conflict emerged and history came to be shaped by the struggle between the consciousnesses of different classes. Thus a sharp distinction is drawn between pre-state and state societies, the determinist view of human consciousness being characteristic of the former but not of the latter.

Two comments are of importance here. First, there is no acceptable anthropological evidence to support such an evolutionary scheme; the reconstruction of a pre-class society having the form described is more the reconstruction of a theoretical antithesis to a class society than a demonstrable stage of human social evolution. Secondly, the postulation of such an evolutionary stage created considerable difficulties for Marxist theory, difficulties which Gottwald has inherited. Marxist theory depended on the contradiction between conflicting groups and classes: the historical process was one of the gradual resolution of that conflict. A pre-class society, however, provided no material for Marxist analysis, and, in particular, allowed for no way of accounting for historical change. So, the transformation of a pre-class into a class society could not be explained. Both these points are directly relevant to Gottwald's reconstruction. His presentation of pre-monarchic Israel, as a classless egalitarian society in which consciousness is determined by social and economic conditions, is precisely parallel to Marx's pre-class society, and, like the latter, is based upon a series of theoretical antitheses to the essential characteristics of the statist system rather than upon any direct evidence. Furthermore, the transition from pre-monarchic to monarchic Israel is not open to explanation in Gottwald's scheme: the development of tribal Israel was, he argues (1980,33) 'aborted by the introduction of the political form of the monarchy'. Gottwald may be justified in using the designation Marxist of his view of pre-monarchic Israel, but it should then be remembered that the aspect of Marxism which he has adopted is not that dialectical materialism which provides a strategy for research, but in fact is a secondary Marxist theoretical postulate which is effectively a dead end so far as the study of history and of social development is concerned.

In the end, therefore, Gottwald has not provided a satisfactory Marxist analysis nor an adequate structural-functionalist analysis of pre-monarchic Israel. The two approaches have been linked to a form of materialism, which, by effectively rejecting dialectic, excludes individual Israelites as real actors on the stage of history. This is true to neither Marx nor Durkheim.

4. The approach of Douglas and Soler towards an understanding of the dietary laws of ancient Israel belongs within the framework of the Durkheim tradition. The more immediate influence on both, however, is Lévi-Strauss, whose structural anthropology is based on the claim that kinship systems, however complex and diverse, exhibit a patterning which reflects the activity of the mind in ordering and classifying, an activity which has the same 'binary' nature as that to be found in the structure of language (see Rogerson:1978,102ff.; Hamnett:1984,211ff.). The ordering of reality in terms of opposition and classification is

argued by Douglas and Soler similarly to lie behind the distinction between clean and unclean animals. In this respect Douglas and Soler may be open to the charge made against Lévi-Strauss (Morris:1987,265ff.) of having deviated from Durkheim by presenting in the end a form of psychological reductionism. Nevertheless, their work still clearly belongs within the framework of structural-functionalist approaches to society and religion and so may appropriately be noted at this point.

Rejecting any explanation of the distinction between clean and unclean based on notions of hygiene, which presupposes that Moses was 'an enlightened public health administrator' (1966:29), Douglas argues that the dietary regulations of Leviticus and Deuteronomy are to be interpreted within the general context of the fact that rules relating to that which is clean and unclean are symbolic systems. For both ancient and modern times the unclean is essentially 'matter out of place'; it is a residual category, comprising that which lies outside our schemes of classification. Such schemes are the patterns into which the perceiver organizes what is perceived. Each of us creates a world by classifying and so bringing order to the phenomena we perceive (*ibid.*,36). That which is unclean is that which cannot be incorporated and does not fit within the system of ordering and classifying.

The injunctions relating to clean and unclean food in Leviticus and Deuteronomy are related to the command to be holy (Lev.11:45; Deut.14:2,21). Holiness implies not only separation but also wholeness; so physical perfection is required of things presented in the temple and of persons approaching it. It also excludes hybrids and confusions: holiness requires that individuals conform to their class, and that different classes of things be not confused. It means keeping distinct the categories of creation, and so involves correct definition, discrimination and order. Cloven-hoofed and cud-chewing ungulates are the model of the proper kind of food for the pastoralist; clean wild game must conform to those characteristics. Unclean species are further defined as those which do not conform to the scheme of creation and its separation of the three elements, water, air and earth. To each element belongs its proper class, and any class of creature not equipped for the right kind of locomotion in its element is not holy and so is unclean. This is the case with anything in the water that has not fins and scales, with four-footed creatures (which properly belong to the earth) that fly, with creeping things on the ground.

In an independent study Soler (1979) reaches remarkably similar conclusions, which are more explicitly linked with the structuralism of Lévi-Strauss. Again noting that there is a link between dietary habits and perception of the world, Soler notes first the general order given in the Pentateuchal narrative where the dietary regulations are contained: paradise was vegetarian, and it was only with the new era, after the cataclysm of the flood, that God assigned also animals as food (Gen.9:3). At this stage there was no distinction between clean and unclean animals, just as no distinction was made between those who did and those who did not stand in covenant with God. It was only when the latter distinction was introduced, with Moses, that a new dietary regime also came into being. To the distinction between men there corresponds a distinction between animals which may or may not be eaten. Through dietary regulations one people is separated off from others. The explanation for these regulations is not to be found in the nature of any particular item of food (*ibid.*,25). Rather, the prohibitions together constitute a system which is to be seen in relation to other systems.

The Hebrew system is built upon the desire to keep as close as possible to God's intention in creation, while making allowance for the killing of animals. So the prohibition of animals which do not have a cloven hoof and do not chew the cud is intended to exclude carnivorous animals, since these are not envisaged in the plan of creation (Gen.1:29f.); a similar intention lies behind the prohibition of eating most of the birds cited as unclean, for they too are carnivorous. Only herbivorous animals are clean. But some of the latter (horse, ass, camel, hare, rock badger) are considered unclean; the reason is that these do not have a foot analogous to the foot of domestic herbivorous animals, cows and sheep, which set the norm. The defining characteristics, used to determine which animals conform to the plan of creation and which do not, are those of the well known herbivorous domestic livestock. Anything which does not show such defining characteristics suffers from a blemish and is unclean. Likewise, any anomaly in relation to the norm in a species constitutes a blemish and is unclean. This is true of men and animals, as well as of substances; that which is changed from its natural state, as leavened bread through fermentation with leaven, is forbidden for the purposes of sacrificial offering.

Clean animals are those which, in conformity with the plan of creation, are vegetarian; they are also those which conform to the ideal, being without blemish. Creation comprises three elements, and the clean animal is that which belongs properly within this scheme, being a part of one element only: the animals of the earth must walk, the fish must swim and the birds must fly, if they are to be clean. Unclean animals do not fit perfectly within the element to which they belong, especially in relation to the organs of movement within that element (*ibid.*, 29). The system, however, is not simply to be seen as derived from the story of creation. Rather, the classification, together with the story of creation, is based on a system of classification in which God, man, animals and plants are defined through their relationships of opposition (*ibid.*, 29).

5. Finally, reference may be made to studies of prophecy and society by Wilson (1980) and Petersen (1981). These do not in the end offer an analysis of social structure within which the prophet functioned, but they do presuppose a functionalist concept of society as a pre-existent reality which in a time of stress and rapid social change produced prophets. Prophets are 'intermediaries', who function as spokesmen for support groups; there were no socially isolated intermediaries. On the basis of the work of Lewis especially, intermediaries may be divided into two groups. These are not absolutely isolated groups, since prophets may be found in now one and now the other context. The peripheral intermediary functions within a socially peripheral or minority group. He effectively helps maintain social stability by providing a dynamic way of alleviating tensions between minority and majority groups. The central intermediary, on the other hand, has a strong political role: he gives guidance for the army in time of war; he regulates the succession at a time of change of ruler; he is political as well as spiritual adviser to the ruler. Usually central intermediation is more conservative than peripheral: it is primarily responsible for maintaining society and promoting community welfare; it provides supernatural legitimation for the existing social order; it is not against change, but is interested in regulating the pace at which change takes place; it can be critical of society, but under the guise of restoring traditional beliefs and attitudes.

Other distinguishing characteristics, noted by Petersen

(1981,51ff.), are these: the pressures leading to the rise of peripheral prophetic cults are internal to society, while those leading to the rise of central prophecy are external; peripheral prophetic cults are fostered in socially underprivileged situations, while central prophecy is part of the central institutions of society; prophetic activity is a group phenomenon in peripheral cult contexts, but this is not the case with central intermediation; central intermediation is closely concerned with morality in society, and the object of its worship is a moral god, while in peripheral cults it is the power rather than the moral nature of the god which is the main concern.

Wilson (1980,135ff.) has applied this paradigm to both extra-biblical and Old Testament instances of prophecy. In pre-classical prophecy, Samuel was a central intermediary as were also Gad and Nathan in David's court, while Ahaziah, Elijah and Micaiah were peripheral; Elisha was a peripheral prophet who possibly became a central prophet with the accession of Jehu. Among the classical prophets, Hosea was a peripheral prophet opposed by the central cult; Amos was possibly a central prophet in the south but was peripheral in the north; Isaiah was a central prophet with ready access to the king, though apparently later he became peripheral, only subsequently, perhaps as a result of Hezekiah's reform, to become central again; Micah was a peripheral prophet opposed to the Jerusalem establishment including its central prophets; Habbakuk was a central prophet whose oracles, however, were apparently not fulfilled, as a result of which he may have begun to have his authority questioned by his support group; Zephaniah was a central prophet who synthesized the Jerusalemite and deuteronomic traditions, and so remained a central prophet; Jeremiah, on the other hand, was a peripheral prophet in conflict with Hananiah; Ezekiel was a Zadokite influenced by Deuteronomy and became a peripheral prophet.

This is a promising line of approach, usefully setting Old Testament prophecy within a much broader perspective, and offering many illuminating individual insights. The nature of society which it presupposes, however, needs to be made much more explicit, in order to give the terms central and peripheral more substantial sociological content (cf. Long:1982,251).

5

Sociology and Old Testament Study

Introduction

The conflict and structural-functionalist traditions in sociology may in the first instance be distinguished by reference to the role which they assign to the individual in society: for the one, the individual is an active creator of the society in which he lives; for the other, society is a given entity which exerts a determinative influence on the individual. This distinction, however, is by no means an absolute one, especially because the conflict tradition certainly does not exclude the reciprocal influence which is exerted back on the individual by the social structure which he creates. Weber's presentation of ancient Israel, in line with his general sociology, understands the individual as one whose thinking is conditioned by the economic and social context to which he belongs.

The two traditions may also, however, be distinguished by other and more distinctive aspects. First, conflict sociology has a diachronic, historical interest, and understands society as a fragile, changing entity subject to the interacting influences of its competing groups; structural-functionalism has a more static, synchronic and non-historical interest, and understands society as a balanced cohesive unit of interlocking segments. Secondly, Weber's sociology is identified not only by reference to the conflict tradition within which it stands, but also by its description as interpretative sociology (cf. Giddens:1971,145ff.). This means that it sees the sociological task as that of understanding the meanings by which individuals organize their environment. The individual is not simply one who in some mechanical way acts to create social structures; rather, he is one who in his perception and understanding of his environment bestows meaning on that environment and acts in accordance with that meaning. This does not imply a psychological reductionism, that all human institutions are to be explained by reference to the psychology of individuals, for individuals are themselves conditioned by social and cultural influences. Nevertheless, social institutions, states, associations, business corporations, should not be reified into having their own independent identity, but must be understood solely in terms of their origins in particular individual actions (Weber:1947,101). In understanding the meaningful actions of individuals, the sociologist can reach an understanding of society. On the other hand, structural-functionalism not only sees society as the given which determines its individual members, but also approaches society in a positivist way as an object to be analysed. Not only is the individual excluded as an active creator of society, but there is little place here for any significance to be attached to the role of the individual as interpreter bringing meaning to his context. Such meanings, and the meaningful action which accompanies them, have in this tradition little if any sociological significance.

A further distinction between the two traditions follows on from this. Interpretative sociology not only reaches out for the meanings which individuals bring to their context, but is concerned with the role of the historian or sociologist as one who also has an interpretative role in his attempt to understand history and society. History and society may have objective existence, but they are known to the historian and sociologist only in a relationship of interpretation, in which the historian and sociologist bring meaning to their data. On the other hand, the positivist approach of structural-functionalism leaves little room for the significance of the interpretative role of the historian or sociologist. History is understood in terms of the reconstruction of the past as an objective exercise in assembling factual information; society is an object to be analysed objectively. This should make clear why 'ideal types' and 'ideology' are characteristic concerns of the interpretative sociological tradition, but not of structural-functionalism: ideal types are the conscious theoretical constructions articulated by the historian as the means by which he reaches a relationship of understanding with the past; ideology is the expression of meaning which an individual or group bestows on its environment. On the other hand, it is also then clear why the positivistic tendency in structural-functionalism should come to expression in the use of models such as 'segmentary society' or 'chieftainship' as objective descriptions of pre-monarchic Israel, or in an emphasis on the environment, geography and climate as determinants of the form that Israel adopted. The biblical record is dismissed as deriving from individualistic bias and prejudice, with no significance for the historical and sociological analysis of ancient Israel, while reliable objective knowledge can be found in sociological models, and archaeological and other non-biblical sources which are thought to yield objective data for historical and sociological description. Much recent work on ancient Israel reflects these interests and concerns of structural-functionalism.

Sociological assumptions in recent Old Testament study

In a recent article Herion (1986) has illustrated how modern social contexts and assumptions shape scholarly pre-understandings of what is generally true of human social life, and consequently limit the number of options available to historians in their reconstructions of the past. The assumptions which are currently operative in Old Testament scholarship, even though they are not unquestioned by the social sciences, are positivism (the only valid form of knowledge is objective knowledge of the kind accepted by the natural sciences), reductionism (the tendency to explain the complex in terms of the simple, as through the use of models), relativism (issues of morality and religion are never totally right or wrong in any absolute sense), and determinism (the tendency to think that human values, choices and actions are determined by certain variables in the social and cultural environment). When the past is understood within a framework formed by these categories, it becomes meaningful and relevant to a modern audience. Thus, Wilson's argument (1980) that the prophet's message is an expression of the internalized values of his support group, behind which may be found socio-political and socio-economic concerns, is held to reflect a relativistic and deterministic outlook; his application of the simple model of the prophet and his support group to complex data where it is inappropriate reflects positivism and reductionism in that the model has become a historical datum rather than simply a heuristic device. As far as Gottwald's study (1980) is concerned, relativism and determinism are held to lie behind his treatment of Israelite religion as a projection of the economic and political interests of society. Positivism and reductionism appear in his presentation of ancient Israel as conforming to all the rules of the macro-sociological theories of Durkheim, Weber and Marx.

Herion has clearly shown that much current Old Testament scholarship works on the basis of certain often unacknowledged cultural and philosophical assumptions. These assumptions are part of the nature of the philosophical and sociological tradition to which Wilson and Gottwald belong or which they have used as the means best suited to their historical task. It is a tradition which clearly has particularly close affinities with the sociological method to be traced back to Durkheim: Israelite society is seen as a total integrated system; the religion of Israel is part of her ideational superstructure, and so is dependably related to her social and economic structure; the role of the individual is weakened to the point of non-existence; the value of Old Testament texts in the reconstruction of Israelite history is diminished; a particular emphasis is placed on archaeology, geography and environment as the basis for objective historical knowledge.

At that point, however, where he presents his own criticism of the outlook of Wilson and Gottwald, Herion has introduced a certain confusion which has important implications for sociological method. Wilson's relativism and determinism are said to have the result that the prophet himself cannot be understood to have had any true sense of 'good' which transcended his group's particular interests, the capacity to believe in absolutes having been removed from the world of ancient Israel (Herion:1986,11). Similarly, Gottwald is criticized for allowing his particular social scientific understanding of religion to determine the religious understanding of the ancient Israelites themselves. The result, argues Herion, is a historical reconstruction unable to concede the Israelite peasants' ability to possess any genuine sense of 'good' transcending their own socio-political goals and socio-economic interests.

The particular problem with this criticism is that in projecting on to ancient Israelites the views of Wilson and Gottwald it confuses a modern social science understanding of the nature and function of religion with what Israelites themselves believed. Wilson and Gottwald do not intend primarily to describe the beliefs of the ancient Israelites; rather, they set out to explain, with the help of sociological theory, the origin and nature of those beliefs in a way which will satisfy contemporary thought.

In a study which relates closely and directly to this issue, Rogerson (1985) has proposed that the sociological methodology advocated by Runciman should be adopted for Old Testament studies. According to Runciman, sociology has different aims and approaches which may be defined in terms of distinct levels. These are the levels of reportage, explanation, description, and evaluation. Reportage is the gathering together of information in value free language. Explanation attempts, through the use of conceptual models, to determine the causes of what is reported, to understand and account for a particular reported situation. The Old Testament scholar, however, suffers from the particular disadvantage that the range of available historical information is so limited; so Old Testament historical reconstruction frequently makes use of conceptual models at an early stage in order to compensate for this lack. Models, however, do properly belong to the level of explanation rather than that of reportage, and their use in Old Testament studies to compensate for the poverty of historical data carries the danger that these two levels of sociological concern will become confused. Thus, for example, the amphictyony, intended as an analogy or model of explanation for pre-monarchic Israel, quickly came to be accepted as a historical datum.

Description is concerned with what it was like to be in a particular society or situation. It can make direct use of the Old Testament to expound what it was like to be a member of the people of Yahweh. The historical accuracy or credibility of the information provided by the Old Testament is not at issue at this point; here, the information is taken as a reflection of the beliefs and attitudes of the ancient Israelites. At this level of description, religion may be described in idealist terms, even though these may be inappropriate at other levels, particularly at the level of explanation. The distinction between the levels of explanation and description is implied in the proposals of Wilson and Gottwald, and when this is recognized the confusion introduced by Herion's criticism may be avoided.

Evaluation involves passing a moral judgment on phenomena

on the basis of the observer's own values, of which, in order to avoid distortion at the other levels, the observer should be consciously aware. So, the observer's preference for prophetic religion over against priestly religion, or his dislike of sacrificial ceremonial, should not determine judgments at the levels of reportage, explanation, or description.

This is an attractive and apparently persuasive approach. What is especially attractive about it at this point is that it avoids the so-called genetic fallacy, the view that the nature, significance and truth of something is to be decided on the basis of an account of its origins. When applied to ancient Israel, Runciman's method allows us to explain the religion of Israel by reference to social and economic factors, while the question of the nature, significance and truth of that religion for ancient Israelites still remains to be decided on the basis of the level of description.

The proposals of Runciman constitute, however, a refinement of sociological method involving certain presuppositions which should be made explicit. Most obviously, perhaps, the isolation of a level of value-free reportage, with reference either to the reconstruction of history or to theorizing about contemporary society, presupposes an objectivism, or at least a degree of objectivism, which could be acceptable only in the most principled of positivistic and empirical contexts. Given the impossibility of reporting all phenomena, such reporting as does take place is based upon selection, and selection can be made only on the basis of explanation and evaluation. These may be unconscious procedures, but none the less real for all that: those events are reported which are important for the reporter, and that judgment is made not simply on the basis of their intrinsic significance, but more particularly on the basis of the reporter's own values and on the basis of an understood synchronic and diachronic framework of explanation and causality. That this is the case with the biblical historians requires no argument; that it is the case also with modern reconstructions of ancient Israelite history has been shown by Sasson's study (1981) of the way in which American and European historians of ancient Israel have been influenced by their own contexts. The possibility of a level of value free reportage is impossible for history; it is no more possible for sociology.

The point may be obvious, but it should be emphasized because it relates directly to the more difficult and yet equally potentially distorting distinction between explanation and description. The distinction made here reflects an underlying philosophical methodology. It is significant that explanation and description are distinct levels which are to be approached in that order. Since the level of description follows on that of explanation, the beliefs of individuals (what it was like to be a member of the people of Yahweh) are effectively excluded as causative factors in the development of the level of explanation; they are confined to a descriptive level which is considered only after explanation has already been concluded. The way is then open to understand the individual in history as the product of his social and economic environment, an environment which may be explained quite independently of that individual's thoughts and intentions, and which is in fact the context and foundation of those thoughts and intentions.

Runciman's methodology is basically a materialistic and positivistic methodology, and, as such, it acts as a good sociological and theoretical framework for the materialistic and positivistic proposals of Wilson and Gottwald. If Wilson and Gottwald are to be criticized, therefore, it must be on the basis of a critique of the method, essentially at this point that of Runciman, which lies behind it. The central issue here, as already indicated, is that the separation of the levels of explanation and description effectively presupposes a particular view of the relationship of the individual to society and to history, by making the individual Israelite's own understanding of his world essentially irrelevant to the task of explaining the origin and nature of that world.

A comparison between the works of Frick, on the one hand, and Coote and Whitelam, on the other, reveals the necessity for a clarification of the presuppositions at work here. Their work on the origins of Israel and the rise of the Israelite state was described in the previous chapter within the context of the same sociological approach, but in one respect there is a difference between them. Frick (1985,197) asserts that 'the environment of early Israel tended to select for those technologies (terraces, etc.) and social organizational structures (segmentary society > chiefdom > state) that could maximize and extend the capabilities of the labor supply'. It may well be true that nature 'selects' within the natural order, but this process is here understood (though this is not generally the case in Frick's study) to extend also directly into the human domain. No discontinuity constituted by human reason or human consciousness is understood to interrupt the immediate involvement of men with their environment. By contrast, Coote and Whitelam (1986,121) have argued that Israel is the name of that political form which achieved and maintained political stability on the basis of a cessation of intergroup conflict, a truce which allowed the exploitation of the highlands for subsistence agriculture as the chosen alternative to continued involvement in the conflicts of the economically declining city-states. While the external and environmental factors were necessary conditions for the rise of Israel and the emergence of the Israelite state, such developments were internal responses to those factors, and so dependent on individual action and decision. The question of the role of human action is central to the sociological issue.

Some recent sociological theory

In a comprehensive critique of what he refers to as naturalistic social science, Giddens (1987,52ff.) has argued that the empirical areas of research in the social sciences have not yet caught up with what is happening in social theory; they continue to work from an old naturalistic perspective, since their methods and objectives are more or less those of natural science. They work, in other words, largely within a positivist and materialist framework. In social theory, however, there is coming into existence a different perspective which integrates strands from English-speaking and continental philosophy. This may be seen in the emerging understanding of the nature of human action. Objectivists who stress society and institutions have failed to deal adequately with the qualities which must be attributed to human agents: self-understanding, intentionality, acting for reasons. Subjectivists, on the other hand, tend to skirt issues concerned with long term processes of change and the large scale organization of institutions. Action is not simply an aggregate of intentions; rather, it has an essential temporality which is part of its constitution and so is related to those concepts, structures and institutions which have been so important for objectivists.

Giddens suggests, therefore, that an appropriate way of understanding the relationship between individual action and society is by using, as an analogy, Saussure's linguistic model of relationship between *langue* and *parole*. The structure of a language consists of relations of absences and presences embedded in the instantiation of language in speech or in texts. That is to say, every act of speaking or writing (*parole*) presupposes, is carried out within the context of, at the same time both creates and yet is made possible by, the structure of the language (*langue*), a structure which is both present and absent in every act of speaking or writing. So, then, in the social context, institutions and societies have structural properties in virtue of the continuity of the actions of their component members; but these members of society are able to carry out their day to day activities only in virtue of their capability of instantiating those structural properties.

Giddens (1987,6ff.) has proposed, therefore, that the notion of human freedom and purposeful action should be maintained with four qualifications. First, individuals act according to the conventions of their milieu. Secondly, most of the knowledge we have of the conventions which define our actions is not only contextual, it is basically practical and *ad hoc*; our discourse about our actions and our reasons for them only touches on certain aspects of what we do in our day to day lives. Thirdly, our activities constantly have consequences that we do not intend and of which we might be quite oblivious when undertaking the behaviour in question; so, while as social agents we are necessarily the creators of social life, social life is at the same time not our own creation. Fourthly, the study of the intertwining of what is intended and what is not is a task of elementary importance in sociology; all action is situated in limited time-space contexts, so all of us are influenced by institutional orders that none of us intentionally established.

This is effectively an argument for a synthesis of the two sociological traditions considered in this study (see also Berger:1966,146ff.): the Durkheim tradition which stresses the objectivity of social reality; the Weber tradition which emphasizes subjective meanings, intentions and interpretations brought into any social situation by the actors who participate in it. It recognizes that while society defines the individual, society is itself defined by the individual. Society exists by virtue of the definition and recognition given to it by individuals. Individual intentions and meaningful actions are, therefore, integral to, though by no means the only factor involved in, the existence of

126

society. This restoration of the individual to his role in society opens the way to an almost overwhelming range of complex issues which then directly impinge on the sociological task. An adequate sociology must then include an adequate understanding of the individual, particularly a psychological understanding. The need for this can never be neglected in favour of the legitimate requirements of the structural-functionalist approach for the consideration of the nature of the collectivities to which the individual belongs.

D. H. Wrong (1977,31ff.) has noted that social theory is a set of answers to questions, and that if the latter are forgotten then the answers tend to become fixed and rigid concepts. The questions were first properly defined by Hobbes: how is order possible and why do men not destroy each other in the pursuit of self-interest? The starting point for understanding man in society was thus man and his individual instincts and drives based on self-interest. More recent sociological study, however, has, Wrong believes, appropriated Freudian psychoanalytic theory, or at least that part of the theory which refers to the individual's internalization of social and cultural norms in the process of socialization. So the starting point of sociology has now come to be society and the social norms which the individual internalizes, and the question with which Hobbes started is now transformed into a different question: how are conflict and deviation possible?

The theory of the internalization of social norms is, however, only part of Freud's psychoanalytic theory; otherwise the theory concerns the individual with his innate drives and instincts, into whose superego or conscience those social norms are integrated. Psychoanalytic theory is fundamentally concerned with the eternal conflict between the superego and the instinctual demands of the id, and neglect of the latter necessarily results in a sociology which can find little room for the individual. On the other hand, psychoanalytic theory has generally been seen as essentially confined to the individual and his psychic constitution, which is undoubtedly at least part of the reason for its neglect by sociologists. For Freud, however, the conflict which he identified at the heart of every individual presupposes man in society, and however much psychotherapy may be directed to the individual, its aim, that of easing the strain imposed by the tension between superego and id, presupposes an understanding of the individual only within society.

Psychoanalytic theory is, therefore, closely related to sociology, and especially to the more recent theoretical work on the nature of human action. Freud and Durkheim agreed that the individual has instincts which are overlaid by conscience, and that the latter is a social product. It was conscience, however, which engaged Durkheim's attention, and as a result he ignored the conflict between the conscience and the id, and indeed also rejected the possibility of introducing psychological explanations into sociology. Durkheim's sociology may be said, therefore, to be concerned with the scientific explanation of human behaviour as a social phenomenon, rather than with its understanding in terms of the individual. Freudian psychoanalysis, as indeed Weberian sociology, is an attempt to overcome that dichotomy (cf. Morris:1987,152f.; Bocock:1976,128ff.); psychoanalytic theory has, therefore, strong links with the interpretative tradition in sociology rooted in Weber. Both Freud and Weber were concerned with instinctual, affective, traditional and charismatic action; both shared the view that the repression of sexual instincts increased the energy directed by individuals into rational achievement (Weber:1948,350; cf. Bocock:1976,137). Psychoanalytic theory should, therefore, form an integral part of an adequate sociology both of the individual and of whole groups.[1]

Sociological theory and Old Testament study

Recent developments in sociological theory should have a direct impact on the study of ancient Israel. In particular, they should affect the currently dominant movement towards a structural-functionalist and materialistic understanding of Israel in explicitly sociological contributions to Old Testament study. The two general areas of sociological concern: the individual and society, religion and society, may serve here as a framework for some concluding comments.

1.a. The criticism and rejection of much current history writing, which is expressed in the work of Whitelam (above,97f.) and Frick (above,101ff.), must be thoroughly scrutinized. Their critique, which is thoroughly materialist and positivist in orientation, is aimed chiefly at the 'great men make history' approach, which looks to the great personalities and the unique events as the prime movers and the most significant elements in historical reconstruction. In materialist theory, even the great personalities are ineffective pawns in a historical process, and it is within this process that the understanding of all events belongs; individuals do not make history, nor do unique events give it meaning. For the materialist, moreover, the available written sources suffer from such idealist distortions, and to follow these sources or to assign them priority is to perpetuate the illusions that the materialist seeks to destroy. It is on these grounds that the materialist approach argues for the priority of the non-biblical sources over against the Bible. Geography, archaeology, the study of climate, become the foundations for reliable, objective history, providing knowledge of the real causes of the historical process.

The critique of materialism will aim to reincorporate the individual as a real actor on the stage of history. This reincorporation must, however, be within the parameters of a theoretical understanding of the nature of human action as sketched out by Giddens. History is made by men, but it is made in response to given environmental conditions and through the medium of contemporary conventions. This should not be understood to imply only that some charismatic personalities are great and strong enough to break through their social structures (Herrmann:1984,267f.); rather, for all individuals their relationship to their social and environmental context is one of response to given conditions through the conventions of their age. The written sources of the Old Testament are indeed idealistic, but their exclusion from the task of historical reconstruction is the exclusion of an integral, constitutive element in social situations, the individual human actor. The restoration to history and society of the individual, even though in a modified role, implies also the restoration of the written record, even if also in qualified form. The necessary qualifications relate not only to the fact that the texts generally do not recognize the role of the environment in the development of social structure, but also to the need for a sensitive awareness of the linguistic forms by which the conventions of the age come to expression in the texts.

b. The conventions of the age are those forms and structures, social and linguistic, which exist as the givens enabling social life to exist. These forms and structures are, in the first instance, human creations, which, however, secondarily come to be perceived as objective realities, and are, in the course of the socialization of the individual, accepted as such. This is true of both linguistic and social forms and structures. This recognition, as far as language and literature are concerned, lies behind the form critical approach: literary forms exist independently of the individuals who use them, and are identifiable with certain social situations. There is certainly need for flexibility here, in terms of appreciating the creative use made of these forms by individuals (cf.Alter:1987,246f.), a point which precisely corresponds with our chief interest here: the place of the individual and of human action in society, and how that place and action are realized in society.

Life in society is life shared with others, and these others are known and reacted to through humanly created and recurrently objectified patterns or schemes, more or less rigid. These others are known 'as a teacher', 'as a student', etc., schematic classifications which serve as the means by which social encounter is ordered. In action one identifies oneself with the role to which that action belongs; subsequently, in reflection on the action, there is no longer such complete identification, so that the role becomes objectified as (partially) independent of the actor. Social structure is the totality of these objectified roles, and by identifying with these roles the individual participates in society. These roles are the means by which institutional order is represented. It is only through the re-enactment by living actors of the roles prescribed by the institution that the institution itself is recurrently realized (Berger and Luckmann:1979,92). This description of the relationship of the individual to society is closely analogous to that presupposed in Giddens' proposal to use the linguistic model in which *parole* stands in relationship with *langue*.

c. Role theory is clearly of fundamental importance to the question of the relationship of the individual to society: roles, played by individuals, are the means by which social structure is established and realized in history. The typifications with which role theory is concerned have much in common with Weber's ideal types, and represent the extension of the latter into the context of interpersonal relationships. The application of the theory to ancient Israel has so far, perhaps inevitably, been very limited. Petersen, however, has noted (1981) one aspect of role theory which may serve to elucidate characteristics of prophetic behaviour. Role theory is concerned not only with roles as the means by which social structure is realized in history and the institutionalization of society takes place, but also with the degree of commitment, identification and intensity with which a person enacts a role. The level of involvement can be plotted on a spectrum marked off in stages ranging from effective non-involvement to bewitchment. Non-involvement reflects the attitude of the lapsed member of a political party or church; next to it is casual role enactment, or routine involvement; more involved is the ritual acting exemplified in the exuberant greeting of a salesperson or the solemn demeanour of funeral personnel; then comes the engrossed acting of one who throws himself into the role and yet maintains his identity; at the next stage comes classical hypnotic role taking, involving a high degree of self-involvement; histrionic neurosis is a still more intense stage which can be marked by psychosomatic disorders; ecstasy is a new order of intense behaviour involving the suspension of voluntary action, together with distinctive physical activity such as speaking in tongues and walking on coals; the most intensive stage of role involvement is that of bewitchment, exemplified in those who believe themselves to be the object of sorcery, witchcraft and magic.

Petersen believes that prophetic behaviour falls within those stages characterized as ritual acting, engrossed acting, classical hypnotic role taking and histrionic neurosis, but that ecstasy represents a stage beyond the levels of involvement normally to be found. Whether or not this particular view of prophetic behaviour is correct, there is clearly some scope here for more comprehensive study of the relationship of the individual to society, from both sociological and psychological perspectives, even if the empirical data for filling out the theory remain slight. Role theory may function, however, as the framework within which to approach the totality of Israel's social structure, understood as comprising a variety of objectified roles through which her social structure was realized and by means of which individual Israelites participated in that society.

d. The playing of a role in society involves not only certain types of action but also the adoption of the norms, values and emotions which belong to that role (Berger and Luckmann:1979,94ff.). Such objectified 'knowledge' becomes the accepted knowledge of the person playing the role. Depending on the role, such knowledge may be highly technical and specialized, or it may be much more general and 'common sense'. In highly differentiated societies, with increasing specializations, the expert in his role will have not only the specific knowledge belonging to his role but also the more general knowledge by which his role relates and makes sense to society at large. In less differentiated societies, in which role-specific knowledge is less developed, the degree of separation between the specific knowledge and the general knowledge will be proportionately less. In such undifferentiated societies, the institutional order is less fragmented, the structure and roles through which institutionalization is historically realized are less specific and more widely shared, so that the knowledge implicit in those structures and roles is more diffused throughout society.

The totality of knowledge in a society constitutes its world view. This, like its structure, is a human creation, that by which individuals make sense of the chaos of impressions which impinge on them. It is a human creation which, again like social structure, comes to assume the status of objective reality, and which is accepted and assimilated by the individual in the course of his socialization as a member of society. The less differentiated the society, the more uniform and comprehensive its world view; the more differentiated the society, the less uniform and comprehensive its world view. In the latter case, the common social base and common stock of knowledge is first of all supplemented by, and then begins to give way to, the knowledge and world view specific to each of society's different segments. This has direct relevance to the study of ancient Israel as to the study of any society: differentiation within society, expressed as differentiation in roles and role specific knowledge, means that society comes to be segmented also with respect to world view. The clash of interests in society will exist then not only on the level of politics and economics but also on the idealist level of world view, and structurally society will remain united to the extent that there remains sufficient accepted common ground both in terms of social, political and economic structures, and in terms of world view.

As roles and knowledge specific to them become esoteric, so

society is segmented into subgroups, each with its own world view. The relationship of such subgroups to the total society, together with the relationship of its knowledge to the wider common knowledge of the society, is a matter of legitimation. So, to use the illustration offered by Berger and Luckmann (*ibid.*,102ff.), the esoteric subgroup of medical experts exists on the basis of convincing both the lay public of its legitimacy in terms of the benefits which it confers on society, and also the medical fraternity of the validity of its practices and standards. If legitimacy is not present, because the subgroup's knowledge is rejected by the rest of society or because it no longer carries conviction for its own members, the status of that subgroup within society is put under severe strain.

From the perspective of those who belong to a group with its own knowledge and world view, a group which has its own understanding of reality, it may be said that the individual's perception of reality depends upon the ongoing support of the social group to which he belongs (Berger and Luckmann, *ibid.*,174). This means that the individual cannot maintain a particular view or understanding of reality in complete isolation; without supporting structures, coming to expression in meeting, conversation, ritual and so on, beliefs lose their quality of objective reality and so also their claim on the individual. The individual understanding of reality is a fragile creation which in such extreme situations may lose all credibility. In less extreme situations, brought about simply by the mutual contact of different groups with different world views, the nature of the effect of such contact on any given world view will depend on a variety of factors relating to the strength and stability of the social groups in question.

This is clearly of immediate general significance for the history and religion of Israel, and particularly for understanding the processes which led to the production of the Old Testament. A beginning has been made in developing an understanding within this framework by Morton Smith's discussion (1971) of the history and interrelationship of the various parties and groups which lie behind the emergence of the partisan materials collected in the Old Testament. An explicit adoption of the social-psychological perspective, however, and a specific illustration of its possible application to the Israelite context, is provided by Carroll's work on the prophets (1977; 1979).

133

e. Carroll has used Festinger's theory of cognitive dissonance as a framework for understanding reactions to failure of expectation or prediction in prophecy. The theory proposes that a state of cognitive dissonance arises when different understandings of reality come into conflict, and that the attempt will be made to reduce or to resolve the conflict by particular identifiable procedures. A state of dissonance does not require the actual meeting of different social groups; it may occur within the context of one group, when, however it may happen, knowledge is made available to it which conflicts with already held belief. In any case, the response to dissonance and the attempt to resolve or reduce it involve rationalization or explanation designed to strengthen already held beliefs or to harmonize them with the new knowledge; also involved is association with others who share already held beliefs, and the avoidance where possible of potential sources of dissonance. Some or all of these procedures may become operative in any given instance of resolution of cognitive dissonance (Carroll:1979,95).

As Carroll (*ibid.*,103ff.) has noted, dissonance theory is not immune to criticism. People do live with conflicting cognitions and feel no need to resolve the dissonance; there may be lack of precision in the theory, in that the reinterpretation of a given prediction may be a classic instance of dissonance response, but alternatively it may be a matter of an improved understanding of the nature of the prediction; the theory is potentially too simplistic in that it is rarely possible to analyse a complex social structure in terms of two conflicting cognitions. Such difficulties apply directly to the biblical context: in the post-exilic community living chiefly by torah, problems of dissonance relating to the prophetic traditions would have been insignificant for most people; any given religious explanation may be a response to dissonance, but it may also be an interpretation of an existing complex faith structure. In addition, there are considerable problems in determining how or in what terms ancient Israelite groups would have been aware of the disconfirmation of prediction, which would have given rise to dissonance, while even if such awareness was present response to it may have remained at the oral level, leaving no trace in the written tradition. Nevertheless, the theory does provide categories which may be transposed into the biblical context as one possible way of examining at least this particular aspect of prophecy. These categories include exclusive social support groups which avoid dissonance arousing ideas, events or experiences, and serve to strengthen the beliefs of their members; they include also the techniques of explanation and rationalization by means of which situations of dissonance are resolved.

The social support group, which functioned to resolve dissonance by providing identity and protection for the individual, may be the context within which to see prophetic communities, and particularly the group of Isaiah's disciples. Carroll's chief interest, however, lies in the techniques of explanation and reinterpretation of prophecy, which are preserved in the prophetic tradition itself and may be understood as responses to dissonance created by failure of expectation or prediction. So, for example, in Isaiah 6, verses 9–10 may be understood as 'a classic response to failure by reinterpretation of original cognition'; that is, the dissonance caused by the general failure of Isaiah's call to repent (Is.1:16,17) is resolved, or reduced, by hermeneutical reflection on his call which concluded that failure was part of his mission (Carroll, *ibid.*, 134ff.). There are many problems associated with this approach, but it remains a good illustration of the positive contribution which a comprehensive social-psychological theory might make to the elucidation of various aspects of Israelite society and religion, and their reflection in the literature of the Old Testament.[2]

2.a. The previous section began as a consideration of the theme individual and society, in the light of some recent sociological study. The critique of materialism led to an understanding of the individual as one who responds to his environment through the conventions of his age. The dialectical relationship implied here, which excludes both pure materialism and pure idealism, acts as a framework within which society may be seen both as that which determines and that which is determined by the individual. In more concrete terms, role theory offers a way of expressing this dialectical relationship, but at the same time this theory also expands the context within which social structure is to be understood. The roles through which social structure is brought into existence embody norms and values, and these constitute the knowledge by which the individual playing the role organizes and understands his place in society, and so brings order to his environment. The knowledge or cognitions of individuals and groups in society, and ultimately of society as a whole, constitute its world view, its understanding of reality. The clash of different cultures, and, within society, the conflict between different classes and groups, include also this cognitive dimension, a dimension which, as far as the Old Testament is concerned, is reflected in records of conflict between prophets, between prophet and society, and also perhaps in those indications of reinterpretation of prophetic oracles.

All of this leads into the specific issue of the relationship between religion and society. Is religion to be understood as world view, the knowledge of society or groups within society, human creation which, like society itself, comes to stand in a dialectical relationship with its creators? If so, then religious belief is human creation pushed to its limits, in the attempt to understand the totality of existence; its relationship to other objectivated structures and beliefs is then to be determined not on the basis of any intrinsic difference, arising from a difference in origin, but on the basis of its comprehensive aim to account for the totality of reality rather than for those aspects of reality which impinge on the individual's immediate social experience.

This is a common way of understanding religion in society. So Geertz proposes that religion is essentially a cultural system which gives meaning to human existence. It is a symbolic system which induces in man uniquely factual and realistic ideas of created order (Geertz:1966,4). Religion gives explanations and emotional support for human suffering, and provides a way of understanding the discontinuity between things as they are and things as they ought to be. The explanatory role of religion and its nature as human projection are also emphasized by Berger (1973), who describes it as the furthest reach of man's self-externalization, in which human order is projected on to the totality of existence in the attempt to conceive of the entire universe as being humanly significant. Since religion is, therefore, like society, in the category of human projection, it necessarily functions in a legitimizing way: both society and religion are human creations bringing order to existence, with religion providing the general justification, in terms of universal order and meaning, for the form which society takes in immediate social experience. This legitimizing relationship of religion to society may be exercised in a mythological way, in the sense that the social order is understood to reflect the divine order in a microcosm-macrocosm relationship, or in terms of divine imperatives, a form of relationship between God and society which arises when, as in Israel, the mythological way of thinking has been broken. In either case, religion is a human creation: it has an explanatory function, in that it brings order to the totality of existence; it has a legitimizing function, in that it sanctions the form which society takes.

b. This phenomenological approach to religion is important in relation to the Marxist materialist critique of religion. It provides a significant response to the charge that religion is an ideological weapon of class domination or a pure subjective illusion based on wish fulfilment, for the conclusion to which it points is that the individual is to be understood as *homo religiosus*, that religious belief belongs to the very nature of man and is not a product of his environment or the ideological expression of his social and economic interests. The concrete forms which religions take may indeed show such influences and betray such interests, but these are but the outward expression of an essential human characteristic which cannot be explained in such terms.

It was in order to strengthen this proposition that Berger later (1970) returned to the topic, in the attempt to show that this religious nature of humanity is not a matter of culture but belongs to the very being of the individual, and, moreover, that it corresponds to that which is ultimately true of the totality of existence. Berger argued that religious phenomena cannot, indeed, be understood to manifest themselves as different from human projections, and that nothing is immune to the relativization of socio-economic analysis. It is only 'in, with and under' the immense array of human projections that indications of a reality that is truly other will be found. Theological thought, however, can and should seek out signals of transcendence within the empirically given human situations. Such signals are constituted by prototypical human gestures, that is, reiterated acts and experiences that appear to express essential aspects of man's being. These may be found in humour, in play, in hope, in absolute condemnation, in all of which the empirically given is transcended; above all, such signals of transcendence may be found in the human propensity for order, grounded in the belief that the created order of society corresponds to an underlying

137

order of the universe, a divine order that supports and justifies all human attempts at ordering, a divine order in the universe in which it makes sense to trust. Human projections, coming to expression in both society and religion, are thus indeed reflections of ultimate reality; religion is then both a human projection and at the same time not simply relative to human social and cultural conditions. It can be understood as the cultural expression of constant human dispositions and attitudes which are themselves reflections of a divine order in reality.

This approach understands religion not only as a cultural expression of meaning, but also as the necessary result of the essentially religious nature of man and the reality in which he lives. In its generalized form, however, it does not account for radical difference between religious systems of meaning and for historical change in those systems; moreover, it seems to suggest a closer correspondence between religious meaning and other forms of meaning, or a more complete integration of religion and culture, than is usually empirically to be found. Religion is a human projection, and one which can come to expression only through given social and cultural forms; the problem is that of finding a theoretical model within which to bring to expression both the necessary similarity of religion and other human projections and yet also the observable differences between them, and also to account for the different forms which religions take as systems of meaning within different societies and different epochs.

c. This is an agenda with a daunting comprehensiveness. One step at least towards the development of an adequate theory has, however, been taken by Theissen in a study (1984) devoted to the nature of religious and scientific thought and the relationship between them. Theissen has argued that evolutionary theory provides an appropriate model for this task. The theory of biological evolution holds that organisms have developed through mutation and selection as a means of achieving a better adaptation to reality. In a parallel way, culture, expressed in science, art and religion, may be understood to have developed different forms in the process of adaptation to reality.[3] Mutation in biological evolution is parallel to innovation in cultural evolution; selection in biological evolution is parallel to adaptation in cultural evolution.

There is an important difference between biological and cultural evolution, however, a difference which human consciousness has introduced. Human consciousness, in protest against the harshness of biological evolution, has made possible adaptive change of behaviour as an alternative to the selective elimination of unsuitable life forms. Within culture, both science and faith are processes of adaptation. Neither science nor faith offers reality in itself; both are interpretations of reality, and to that extent reflect processes of adaptation to reality. Reality itself is 'other' and mysterious; to it we bring *a priori* thought categories which in human experience have proved successful in the process of human adaptation to reality.

Evolutionary theory confirms that the mysterious reality to which we are related in all our structures of adaptation is a single, central reality, which gradually and under various aspects discloses itself to us. Knowledge and faith agree in these: first, that behind the world which we interpret there is an intrinsic reality which we cannot yet grasp adequately; secondly, that our life is a structure of adaptation to this reality which is partly successful; thirdly, that all attempts at adaptation relate to a single, central reality. From the rationality of our brain it can further be argued that the reality which makes its evolution possible is itself rational. Faith is the attempt to understand the whole of life as a response to that ultimate reality.

Ultimate reality is more than a productive force, however; in sickness and death, in permitting ways of life to emerge and culminate in historical catastrophe, ultimate reality also shows itself as the merciless pressure of selection. So, this central reality is the creator of the limited world in which we live, which takes shape in adaptation to it. Science and faith can both affirm this reality as a productive force, because it calls forth from both responses which overcome its harshness. Science and faith are different in important ways: science works with hypotheses and the falsification principle and delights in dissent, while religion is apodictic, contravening the facts and depending on consent; science is quick and direct and oriented to the future, while religion is slow and halting and oriented to the past. Despite these differences, however, the responses of science and faith are to be understood as parallel experimental attempts at adaptation to ultimate reality, responses which experience unplannable mutations. In science, the new paradigm which is

139

a mutation of our cognitive structures can hardly be planned; in religion, charismatic revealers such as Jesus, Buddha and Muhammed introduced mutations which have proved themselves to their adherents over centuries.

Through adaptation, in science by the surrender of false hypotheses, and in faith by change in forms of behaviour, the effects of merciless selection on individuals are mitigated. This is the new thing that human consciousness has introduced into evolution, bringing evolution to a new level. The reduction of selection by culture takes place also through differentiation, the provision for a far greater variation in forms of life than is possible in the natural environment. These variations relate to abilities, interests and values, in the fostering of which culture shows a tolerance corresponding to an unimaginable tolerance in ultimate reality. Culture in general reduces selection in this way; religion, at the heart of human culture, is a protest against the principle of selection.

Monotheistic religion belongs in the history of the human attempt to achieve an adequate adaptation to ultimate reality. As such, it is a protest against the principle of selection, resistance to which is characteristic of all culture. In Israel, monotheism was achieved through conflict over the exclusiveness of Yahweh in the pre-exilic period, over his uniqueness in the exilic period, and over his universality in the meeting with Hellenistic philosophical monotheism. It was not the result of a continuous development, but appeared suddenly as a spiritual mutation, a revolutionary transformation of consciousness, a mutation of our religious structures of adaptation to the ultimate reality. Biblical monotheism is a protest against polytheism; it is also a protest against harshness in selection which polytheism tends to tolerate. As long as there are national gods, war between nations can be conceived of as built into the structure of reality; biblical monotheism embraces the vision of a future without war. Polytheism within societies may legitimate exploitation; biblical monotheism is a demand for social justice and equality. Biblical monotheism, in rejecting an identification of God with any one aspect of reality and in prohibiting images, is an affirmation of God as the reality behind the world, who supports, yet is not identical with, nature and society.

Theissen's study is a demanding and suggestive approach towards developing a view of religion in society which gets beyond the dead end discussion of their relative priority and mutual influences, towards a fresh understanding of their interrelationship in a wider context. Religion is a human projection, a construction which belongs in the framework of an evolving culture; its relationship with other cultural forms, such as science and art, is one of identity and difference, the identity arising from their common structure as response to ultimate reality, their difference lying in the methods and forms by which that reality is interpreted. In itself, however, Theissen's study has a strong idealistic emphasis: religion, science and art are the fruit of man's intellectual endeavour to adapt to ultimate reality. Into this context it is clearly necessary to introduce those conventional forms and structures which are the means by which response to ultimate reality comes to expression. Theissen has opened the way for this further development of his approach by noting that

> before any experience whatsoever we are pre-programmed to arrange our impressions according to space and time, to look for causal connections, to note evocative forms and to combine them in analogies. Such pre-programmed patterns of assimilation – the *a priori* elements in our experiences – are the results of genealogical development in which environmental factors select the best attempts at adaptation from the many which have arisen by chance (Theissen:1984,20).

It is in the description of the formation and the nature of these *a priori* elements in the experience of ancient Israel that the sociological approach to the Old Testament has so much to contribute.

Notes

Introduction

1. Good general introductions to sociological study are provided by Berger:1966; Nisbet:1967; Berger and Kellner:1982.

Chapter 1

1. On the term cf. Weber:1948,139. Rationalization means the abolition of mystery and magic, the disenchantment of the world. Rational calculation and technical competence are the way to understanding.
2. Hanson's more recent substantial study (1986) came to notice too late for inclusion. A detailed treatment of it would belong within the context of the *Gemeinschaft-Gesellschaft* typology under consideration in this chapter.
3. Kovacs' questioning of the relationship between literature and social context has serious implications for much Old Testament study. Crüsemann (1978), for example, argues that the anti-monarchic texts of the Old Testament are to be led back to the period of the united monarchy and understood to reflect the interests of a wealthy class of peasant farmer, whose prosperity is put at risk by monarchic demands. Pro-monarchic stories, such as the history of the rise of David and the Joseph story, are counter propaganda, while the Yahwist and the Succession Narrative represent a mediating position. In a similar study of Koheleth, Crüsemann (1984) explains the rejection of the old wisdom principle of the link between act and consequence and the withdrawal into individualism by arguing that traditional wisdom reflects the outlook of a rich landed upper class, while Koheleth's cynicism and individualism reflect the social and economic upheavals accompanying the destruction of Judah;

these events brought to an end the independence and self-sufficiency of that group, and rendered meaningless the old Yahwistic tradition. In much the same way, Brueggemann's discussion (1985) of the sociological framework within which Old Testament thinking on the justice of Yahweh is to be interpreted, presupposes that direct correlation between social situation and literary expression whick Kovacs has questioned.

Chapter 2

1. Marx's critical discussion of Feuerbach is in part concerned with the latter's 'deterministic philosophical materialism', cf. Giddens:1971,20ff. For a discussion of the question of lack of unity in Marx's thought, cf. Giddens:1987,257ff.; on the relationship of Weber and Marx, cf. Wrong:1977, 250ff.
2. For more recent discussion of the place of historical change in structural-functionalist approaches to society, cf. Bellah:1959; Lenski:1976.
3. Robertson Smith was himself influenced by the writings of Fustel de Coulanges, one of Durkheim's teachers. Durkheim was apparently at first critical of the latter's presentation of the central role of religion in the formation of ancient social structures and institutions; cf. Lukes:1975,61ff.; Collins:1985,136ff.; Morris:1987,112. For the influence of Robertson Smith on Durkheim, cf. Jones:1977; Evans-Pritchard:1965,51ff.; and especially Beidelman:1974, whose account is followed here.

Chapter 3

1. 'Das antike Judentum', *Archiv für Sozialwissenschaft und Sozialforschung*, 1917–19, reprinted in *Gesammelte Aufsätze zur Religionssoziologie* vol.III, 1921. English translation, 1952, by H. H. Gerth and D. Martindale.
2. See also Weber:1965,108ff. Weber has been criticized on the two methodological points that have appeared so far. First, it has been argued that his 'teleological' approach, in which he begins by defining the Jewish community and then turns to historical reconstruction to explain its origins,

justifies its explanations in terms of the telos rather than in relation to the successive sets of circumstances which make up the whole historical sequence, and so prejudices the selection of which are the significant factors; cf. Rogerson: 1985,253. Given, however, that no historical description can give a meaningful account of total sets of circumstances without selection, this objection can have only limited validity; if Weber is to be criticized in this context, it should be for the particular telos which he has chosen rather than for the method as such. See also Fahey:1982,63, who notes that for Weber the decisive questions are: what constitutes and determines the particular form that the Israelite religious development took? (Weber:1952,428). Secondly, the term 'pariah people' has been rejected not only as a pre-emptive and value loaded term, but also as lacking a sufficient historical basis and as representing the transfer of the designation of one unique historical phenomenon to another unique historical phenomenon (Schmueli:1968,182ff.; cf. also Guttmann:1925,219f.). There may well be a problem here, but it scarcely affects Weber's methodology as such. One can over-emphasize the uniqueness of each of the situations described, and, given the qualifications which Weber himself attached to the use of 'pariah people' for the Jewish community, it may still be acceptable (as an ideal type) as a useful perspective from which to approach the particular case of ancient Judaism.

3. Schäfer-Lichtenberger:1983,49–106,195–322, provides a comprehensive treatment of the type of the city, covering Weber's sociological study of the city in his earlier writings, and the problems associated with the application of the type to ancient Israel.

4. The role of the Levites in the structure of Weber's study was early criticized by Guttmann:1925,215ff; but even he acknowledged that if the Levites did not provide such religious leadership in pre-prophetic times, some such leadership must nevertheless have existed.

5. This apparent inconsistency in Weber is reflected also in a summary of his thinking on the prophets such as that given by Raphael, who understands Weber to argue that the rationalistic prophetic theodicy eliminates the question of meaning from the universe and history (Raphael:1973,51);

a rational theodicy necessarily involves rather than eliminates questions of meaning.

6. Weber characterized the prophetic ethic as plebeian, that is, a morality which can satisfy the needs of a socially oppressed class; for a criticism cf. Guttmann:1925,220f., who believes that such a characterization takes no account of the heroic trait in the prophetic morality of humility, in which consciousness of doing God's will gives the prophet courage to oppose the authorities.

7. Cf. also Lang:1985,83ff., who argues that peasant communities are not independent but represent only half a society, the other half comprising a propertied, educated and merchant élite, often resident in towns and in control of public affairs. The ruling class is in a position to exploit agricultural production as a result of peasants' running into debt through bad harvests and becoming dependent on urban money lenders and merchants. An older patronage type of peasant–landlord relationship, in which the landlord had obligations towards the tenant in adverse conditions, was, by the time of the eighth-century prophets, replaced by a relationship of exploitation, known as rent capitalism, in which the landlord was interested only in profit making. In the case of both Thiel and Lang it is acknowledged that while such divisions increased under the monarchy, it is a distortion to think of Israel in the pre-monarchic period as a classless and egalitarian society.

8. Mannheim indeed thought in terms of the analysis of the various social influences as a way towards progressively clarifying the object of thought, but this could hardly be taken to justify the idea that by peeling away such social influences a pure and undetermined thought is reached. For a discussion, cf. Berger and Luckmann:1979,20ff.

9. Williams:1969,153ff., has made a scarcely successful attempt to counter Berger's conclusions in the interests of re-emphasizing prophetic independence.

Chapter 4

1. The description which Causse goes on to give corresponds, however, to a society of which Durkheim used the term 'mechanical solidarity'.

2. Reuss was a predecessor of Causse in Strasbourg; he had studied in Germany, and introduced this aspect of evolutionary historical criticism into French biblical scholarship. For the background, cf. especially Kimbrough:1978,17ff., whose comprehensive evaluation of Causse is followed here.

3. In so far as 'pre-logical' thinking does not distinguish between the natural and the supernatural, it is a term which cannot be used of Israel; cf. Rogerson:1977,67ff., who argues that Israel did perceive nature as following its own 'natural' laws, and so saw a difference between natural and supernatural events. For other criticisms of Lévy-Bruhl, see especially Evans-Pritchard:1965,78ff.

4. Lenski:1980,275. Cf. also Brueggemann:1983,174.

5. Much of Gottwald's social analysis finds earlier presentation in de Geus:1976; for both, nomadism is a secondary formation based on a settled way of life; for both, the smallest Israelite unit is the exogamous household, a number of which are found in the endogamous clan; for both, the tribe is a geographical unit. De Geus's definition of the totality of Israel in terms of *connubium* and *forum* is, indeed, preferable to Gottwald's much more vague Israelite federation. Gottwald is, however, treated extensively here rather than de Geus, because of the much more explicitly sociological nature of his treatment.

6. Numerous reviews of Gottwald's book have appeared. Four of these, though not including the two referred to here, have been collected in Gottwald:1983[b],166ff. See also Mayes:1981; 1988.

7. The anthropomorphic material relevant to the discussion of Israel as a segmentary society is now conveniently collected in Sigrist and Neu:1988.

8. The issue of the economic and military background to the rise of the Israelite state is treated more briefly in Gottwald:1983[c],25ff.

9. Frick's highly illuminating and persuasive account of the relationship between egalitarian society, chiefdom and state, could perhaps be supplemented by the point that while the economy of a chiefdom is a distributive economy controlled by the chief, the economy of a state, at least in its fully developed form, is a free market economy in which trade plays a dominant role; for markets in the ancient Near East, cf. Silver:1985.

10. Another model which Frick mentions as particularly suggestive for Israel, though without discussing it in detail, is Renfrew's catastrophe theory, according to which sudden changes or discontinuities in a socio-cultural system are produced by gradual and continuous change in the variables within a system; this provides an alternative to the invasion explanation for change and discontinuity through an analysis of the processes within culture. After the catastrophe of system collapse, according to Renfrew, there first emerges a segmentary society, to be followed by a chiefdom and then a state.

11. It must be doubted that structural-functionalism is quite so non-historical as Gottwald asserts. For the view that there is in fact no such thing as a purely synchronic sociological explanation, cf. Runciman:1973,192.

12. The following critique of Gottwald is heavily dependent on the criticism of Harris in Bloch:1983. On the relationship of idealism and materialism in Marx, cf. also Giddens: 1971,xv,21ff.; McLellan:1980,136f.

Chapter 5

1. On the foregoing see especially Bocock. Both Wrong (1977,31ff.) and Gay (1985) offer persuasive arguments for a psychoanalytic dimension in historical and sociological study. Following Freud's belief that not only individuals but groups and peoples may also be studied from a psychoanalytic view point, it is clear that the theory should not be limited to the study of individual human behaviour in history. For a more critical account, however, which assigns only a limited value to psychoanalytic approaches in history, cf. Lloyd-Jones:1985.

2. Mettinger (1982) has provided another illuminating use of the cognitive dissonance theory: it is the tension between the theology of the presence and protection of Yahweh, on the one hand, and the disastrous historical experience of 586 BC, on the other, which lies behind the emergence of the deuteronomistic theology of the 'name', and the priestly theology of the 'glory', of Yahweh. These theologies provided the means by which faith might be reinterpreted and maintained in the face of disconfirmation.

3. Bowker's study (1973) of the universality and diversity of the forms of human senses of God shares some significant features with Theissen's approach. Bowker argues that religious beliefs should be analyzed in terms of their relationship to 'compounds of limitation', that is, those limitations, especially death, disease and the future, which bound the range of possibility in the construction of forms of human living. Religions are the consequences of projected ways through the limitations which circumscribe human activity (*ibid.*,64f.). It should not pass unnoticed that, like Theissen, Bowker (*ibid.*,59f.) uses the analogy of 'natural selection' in order to describe the relationship between religions and the compounds of limitation over against which they come to expression.

Bibliography

Alt, A.
  1966   *Essays on Old Testament History and Religion*. Oxford:
         Blackwell.
Alter, R.
  1987   'Psalms', pp. 244–62 in *The Literary Guide to the Bible*,
         ed. R. Alter and F. Kermode. London:Collins.
Andersen, F. I.
  1966   'The Socio-Juridical Background of the Naboth
         Incident', *JBL* 85:46–57.
Anderson, B. W.
  1985   'Biblical Theology and Sociological Interpretation',
         Theology Today 42:292–306.
Aron, R.
  1970   *Main Currents in Sociological Thought* 2. Harmondsworth:
         Penguin.
Bächli, O.
  1977   *Amphiktyonie im Alten Testament. Forschungsgeschichtliche
         Studie zur Hypothese von Martin Noth*. Basel:Friedrich
         Reinhardt Verlag.
Beidelman, T. O.
  1974   *W. Robertson Smith and the Sociological Study of Religion*.
         Chicago:University of Chicago Press.
Bellah, R. N.
  1959   'Durkheim and History', *ASR* 24:447–61.
Bellefontaine, E.
  1987   'Customary Law and Chieftainship: Judicial Aspects
         of 2 Samuel 14.4–21', *JSOT* 38:47–72.
Bendix, R.
  1960   *Max Weber: an intellectual portrait*. New York:Doubleday.
Berger, P.
  1963   'Charisma and Religious Innovation. The Social
         Location of Israelite Prophecy', *ASR* 28:940–50.

1966   *Invitation to Sociology.* Harmondsworth:Penguin.

1970   *A Rumour of Angels.* Harmondsworth:Penguin.

1973   *The Social Reality of Religion.* Harmondsworth: Penguin (= US *The Sacred Canopy*, 1967).

Berger, P. and Kellner, H.

1982   *Sociology Reinterpreted: an essay on method and vocation.* Harmondsworth:Penguin.

Berger, P. and Luckmann, T.

1979   *The Social Construction of Reality.* Harmondsworth: Penguin.

Bloch, M.

1983   *Marxism and Anthropology.* Oxford:Oxford University Press.

Bocock, R.

1976   *Freud and Modern Society.* Walton-on-Thames:Nelson.

Bowker, J.

1973   *The Sense of God. Sociological, anthropological and psychological approaches to the origin of the sense of God.* Oxford:Clarendon Press.

Brandfon, F. R.

1981   'Norman Gottwald on the Tribes of Yahweh', *JSOT* 21:101–10.

Brett, M. G.

1987   'Literacy and Domination: G. A. Herion's sociology of history writing', *JSOT* 37:15–40.

Bright, J.

1981   *A History of Israel*[3]. London:SCM.

Brueggemann, W.

1979   'Trajectories in Old Testament Literature and the Sociology of Ancient Israel', *JBL* 98:161–85.

1983   Review of N. K. Gottwald, *The Tribes of Yahweh*, pp. 173–81 in *The Bible and Liberation. Political and Social Hermeneutics*, ed. N. K. Gottwald. Maryknoll:Orbis Books.

1985   'Theodicy in a Social Dimension', *JSOT* 33:3–25.

Buccellati, G.

1967   *Cities and Nations of Ancient Syria.* Studi Semitici 26. Rome:University of Rome.

Carroll, R. P.

1977   'Ancient Israelite Prophecy and Dissonance Theory', *Numen* 24:135–51.

1979   *When Prophecy Failed*. London:SCM.
Caspari, W.
1922   *Die Gottesgemeinde von Sinai und das nachmalige Volk
        Israel*. Beiträge zur Forderung Christlicher Theologie
        27/1. Gütersloh:Bertelsmann.
Causse, A.
1937   *Du groupe ethnique à la communauté religieuse: le problème
        sociologique de la religion d'Israël*. Etudes d'histoire et
        de philosophie religieuses 33. Paris:Felix Alcan.
Chaney, M. L.
1983   'Ancient Palestinian Peasant Movements and the
        Formation of Premonarchic Israel', pp. 39–90 in
        Palestine in Transition, ed. D. N. Freedman and D. F.
        Graf. Sheffield:Almond.
1986   'Systemic Study of the Israelite Monarchy', *Semeia*
        37:53–76.
Collins, R.
1985   *Three Sociological Traditions*. New York:Oxford
        University Press.
Coote, R. B. and Whitelam, K.
1986   'The Emergence of Israel. Social transformation and
        state formation following the decline in Late Bronze
        Age trade', *Semeia* 37:107–47.
1987   *The Emergence of Early Israel in Historical Perspective*.
        Sheffield:Almond.
Crüsemann, F.
1978   *Der Widerstand gegen das Königtum*. WMANT 49.
        Neukirchen-Vluyn:Neukirchener Verlag.
1984   'The Unchangeable World: the "crisis of wisdom"
        in Koheleth', pp. 57–77 in *God of the Lowly. Socio-
        historical Interpretations of the Bible*, ed. W. Schottroff
        and W. Stegemann. Maryknoll:Orbis Books.
Dietrich, W.
1979   *Israel und Kanaan. Vom Ringen zweier Gesellschaftssysteme*.
        Stuttgarter Bibelstudien 94. Stuttgart:Verlag
        Katholisches Bibelwerk.
Douglas, M.
1966   *Purity and Danger. An Analysis of the Concepts of Pollution
        and Taboo*. London:Routledge & Kegan Paul.
Durkheim, E.
1933   *The Division of Labor in Society* (translated by George

Simpson from the 1st [1893] and 5th [1926] editions of *De la division du travail social*). New York:Free Press.

1964   *The Rules of Sociological Method* (translated by S. A. Solovay and J. H. Mueller, from *Les règles de la méthode sociologique* [1895]). New York:Free Press.

1976   *The Elementary Forms of the Religious Life*[2] (translated by J. W. Swain, from *Les formes élémentaires de la vie religieuse* [1912]). London:George Allen & Unwin.

Evans-Pritchard, E. E.
1965   *Theories of Primitive Religion.* Oxford:Clarendon Press.

Fahey, T.
1982   'Max Weber's Ancient Judaism', *AJS* 88:62–87.

Fenton, S.
1984   *Durkheim and Modern Sociology.* Cambridge:Cambridge University Press.

Fiensy, D.
1987   'Using the Nuer Culture of Africa in Understanding the Old Testament. An Evaluation', *JSOT* 38:73–83.

Fishbane, M.
1985   *Biblical Interpretation in Ancient Israel.* Oxford:Clarendon Press.

Flanagan, J. W.
1981   'Chiefs in Israel', *JSOT* 20:47–73.

Fohrer, G.
1971   'Zur Einwirkung der gesellschaftlichen Struktur Israel auf seine Religion', pp. 169–85 in *Near Eastern Studies in Honor of W. F. Albright*, ed. H. Goedicke. Baltimore:Johns Hopkins Press.

1973   *History of Israelite Religion.* London:SPCK.

Frick, F. S.
1977   *The City in Ancient Israel.* SBL Dissertation Series 36. Missoula:Scholars Press.

1985   *The Formation of the State in Ancient Israel.* The Social World of Biblical Antiquity Series, 4. Sheffield: Almond.

Frick, F. S. and Gottwald, N. K.
1983   'The Social World of Ancient Israel', pp. 149–65 in *The Bible and Liberation. Political and Social Hermeneutics*, ed. N. K. Gottwald. Maryknoll:Orbis Books.

Gay, P.
  1985   *Freud for Historians.* Oxford:Oxford University Press.
de Geus, C. H. J.
  1976   *The Tribes of Israel. An investigation into some of the presuppositions of Martin Noth's amphictyony hypothesis.* Assen:van Gorcum.
de Geus, J. K.
  1982   'Die Gesellschaftskritik der Propheten und die Archäologie', *ZDPV* 98:50–7.
Giddens, A.
  1971   *Capitalism and Modern Social Theory: an analysis of the writings of Marx, Durkheim and Max Weber.* Cambridge:Cambridge University Press.
  1977   *Studies in Social and Political Theory.* London: Hutchinson.
  1987   *Social Theory and Modern Sociology.* Oxford:Polity Press.
Gottwald, N. K.
  1979   'Sociological Method in the Study of Ancient Israel', pp. 69–81 in *Encounter with the Text: form and history in the Hebrew Bible,* ed. M. J. Buss. Philadelphia:Fortress Press.
  1980   *The Tribes of Yahweh. A Sociology of the Religion of Liberated Israel, 1250–1050 B.C.E.* London:SCM.
  1983[a] 'Two Models for the Origins of Ancient Israel: Social Revolution or Frontier Development', pp. 5–24 in *The Quest for the Kingdom of God. Studies in Honor of George E. Mendenhall,* ed. H. B. Huffmon, F. A. Spina, A. R. W. Green. Winona Lake: Eisenbrauns.
  1983[b] *The Bible and Liberation. Political and Social Hermeneutics,* ed. N. K. Gottwald. Maryknoll:Orbis Books.
  1983[c] 'Early Israel and the Canaanite Socio-economic System', pp. 25–37 in *Palestine in Transition. The Emergence of Ancient Israel,* ed. D. N. Freedman and D. F. Graf. The Social World of Biblical Antiquity Series, 2. Sheffield:Almond.
Guttmann, J.
  1925   'Max Webers Soziologie des antiken Judentums', *MGWJ* 69:195–223.

Hahn, H. F.
  1966   *The Old Testament in Modern Research*. Philadelphia:
         Fortress Press.
Hamnett, J.
  1984   'Durkheim and the Study of Religion', pp. 202–18
         in *Durkheim and Modern Sociology*, ed. S. Fenton.
         Cambridge:Cambridge University Press.
Hanson, P. D.
  1979   *The Dawn of Apocalyptic*. Philadelphia:Fortress Press.
  1986   *The People Called. The Growth of Community in the Bible*.
         New York: Harper & Row.
Hauer, C.
  1986   'From Alt to Anthropology: the Rise of the Israelite
         State', *JSOT* 36:3–15.
Herion, G. A.
  1981   'The Role of Historical Narrative in Biblical
         Thought. The Tendencies underlying Old
         Testament Historiography', *JSOT* 21:25–57.
  1986   'The Impact of Modern and Social Scientific
         Assumptions on the Reconstruction of Israelite
         History', *JSOT* 34:3–33.
Herrmann, S.
  1984   'King David's State', pp. 261–75 in *In the Shelter
         of Elyon: Essays in Ancient Palestinian Life and Literature
         in Honor of G. W. Ahlström*, ed. W. Boyd Barrick and
         J. R. Spencer. JSOT Supplement Series 31.
         Sheffield:Department of Biblical Studies.
Jones, R. A.
  1977   'On Understanding a Sociological Classic', *AJS*
         83:279–319.
Kimbrough, S. T.
  1972   'A Non-Weberian Sociological Approach to Israelite
         Religion', *JNES* 31:195–202.
  1978   *Israelite Religion in Sociological Perspective. The Work of
         Antonin Causse*. Studies in Oriental Religions, 4.
         Wiesbaden:Harrassowitz.
Kovacs, B. W.
  1976   *Contributions of Sociology to the Study of the Development
         of Apocalypticism: a theoretical survey*. St Louis:SBL
         Consultation on the Social World of Ancient
         Israel.

Kraus, H. J.
1972 'Die Anfänge der religionssoziologische Forschungen in der alttestamentlichen Wissenschaft', pp. 296–310 in *Biblisch-theologische Aufsätze*. Neukirchen-Vluyn: Neukirchener Verlag.

Lang, B.
1983 *Monotheism and the Prophetic Minority*. Sheffield: Almond.
1984 'Max Weber und Israels Propheten', *ZRGG* 36: 156–65.
1985 'The Social Organization of Peasant Poverty in Biblical Israel', pp. 83–99 in *Anthropological Approaches to the Old Testament*, ed. B. Lang. London:SPCK.

Lemche, N. P.
1985 *Early Israel*. VTS XXXVII. Leiden:Brill.

Lenski, G.
1976 'History and Social Change', *AJS* 82:548–64.
1980 Review of N. K. Gottwald, *The Tribes of Yahweh*. *Religious Studies Review* 6/4:275–78.

Lévy-Bruhl, L.
1965 *The 'Soul' of the Primitive* (translated by L. A. Clare from *L'âme primitive* [1927]). London:George Allen & Unwin.

Lloyd-Jones, H.
1985 'Psychoanalysis and the Study of the Ancient World', pp. 152–80 in *Freud and the Humanities*, ed. P. Horden. London:Duckworth.

Long, B.O.
1977 'Prophetic Authority as Social Reality', pp. 3–20 in *Canon and Authority*, ed. G. W. Coats and B. O. Long. Philadelphia:Fortress Press.
1982 'The Social World of Ancient Israel', *Int* 36:243–55.

Lukes, S.
1975 *Emile Durkheim. His Life and Work. A historical and critical study*. Harmondsworth:Penguin.

McLellan, D.
1980 *The Thought of Karl Marx*². London:Macmillan.

Malamat, A.
1976 'Charismatic Leadership in the Book of Judges', pp. 152–68 in *Magnalia Dei. The Mighty Acts of God. Essays*

on the Bible and Archaeology in Memory of G. Ernest
Wright, ed. F. M. Cross, W. E. Lemke and P. D.
Miller. New York:Doubleday.

Malina, B.
  1982   'The Social Sciences and Biblical Interpretation', *Int*
        37:229–42.

Marx, K.
  1977   *Selected Writings*, ed. D. McLellan. Oxford:Oxford
        University Press.

May, H. G.
  1944   'A Sociological Approach to Hebrew Religion', *JBR*
        12:98–106.

Mayes, A. D. H.
  1974   *Israel in the Period of the Judges*. Studies in Biblical
        Theology, Second Series, 29. London:SCM.
  1981   Review of N. K. Gottwald, *The Tribes of Yahweh*. *JTS*
        32:472–83.
  1985   *Judges*. Old Testament Guides. Sheffield:JSOT
        Press.
  1988   'Idealism and Materialism in Weber and Gottwald',
        Proceedings of the Irish Biblical Association 11:44–58.

Mendenhall, G. E.
  1973   *The Tenth Generation. The Origins of the Biblical
        Tradition*. Baltimore:Johns Hopkins University
        Press.
  1975   'The Conflict between Value Systems and Social
        Control', pp. 169–80 in *Unity and Diversity. Essays
        in the History, Literature and Religion of the Ancient Near
        East*, ed. H. Goedicke and J. J. M. Roberts.
        Baltimore:Johns Hopkins University Press.
  1976   'Social Organization in Early Israel', pp. 132–51
        in *Magnalia Dei. The Mighty Acts of God. Essays on the
        Bible and Archaeology in Memory of G. Ernest Wright*,
        ed. F. M. Cross, W. E. Lemke and P. D. Miller.
        New York:Doubleday.

Mettinger, T. N. D.
  1982   *The Dethronement of Sabaoth. Studies in the Shem and
        Kabod Theologies*. Coniectanea Biblica Old Testament
        Series 18. Lund:CWK Gleerup.

Miller, P. D.
  1976   'Faith and Ideology in the Old Testament', pp.

464 – 79 in *Magnalia Dei. The Mighty Acts of God. Essays on the Bible and Archaeology in Memory of G. Ernest Wright*, ed. F. M. Cross, W. E. Lemke and P. D. Miller. New York:Doubleday.

Morris, B.
1987   *Anthropological Studies of Religion.* Cambridge: Cambridge University Press.

Nisbet, R.
1967   *The Sociological Tradition.* London:Heinemann.

Noth, M.
1930   *Das System der zwölf Stämme Israels.* BWANT IV/1. Stuttgart:Kohlhammer.
1948   *Überlieferungsgeschichte des Pentateuch.* Stuttgart: Kohlhammer.
1950   'Das Amt des "Richters Israels" ', pp. 404 – 17 in *Festschrift Alfred Bertholet*, ed. W. Baumgartner, O. Eissfeldt, K. Elliger, L. Rost. Tübingen:J. C. B. Mohr.
1960   *The History of Israel*^{2}. Edinburgh:A. & C. Black.

Otto, E.
1976   'Silo und Jerusalem', *ThZ* 32:65 – 77.
1981   'Sozialgeschichte Israels. Probleme und Perspektiven. Ein Diskussionspapier', *BN* 15:87 – 92.
1988   *Wandel der Rechtsbegründungen in der Gesellschaftsgeschichte des antiken Israel. Eine Rechtsgeschichte des "Bundesbuches" Ex XX 22 – XXIII 13.* Studia Biblica III. Leiden:E. J. Brill.

Overholt, T. W.
1982   'Prophecy: The Problem of Cross-Cultural Comparison', *Semeia* 21:55 – 78.
1984   'Thoughts on the Use of "Charisma" in Old Testament Studies', pp. 287 – 303 in *In the Shelter of Elyon: Essays in Ancient Palestinian Life and Literature in Honor of G. W. Ahlström*, ed. W. Boyd Barrick and J. R. Spencer. JSOT Supplement Series 31. Sheffield:Department of Biblical Studies.

Parsons, T.
1944   'The Theoretical Development of the Sociology of Religion', *Journal of the History of Ideas* 5:176 – 90.

Petersen, D. L.
1979   'Max Weber and the Sociological Study of Ancient Israel', *Sociological Inquiry* 49:117 – 49.

1981   *The Roles of Israel's Prophets*. JSOT Supplement Series
        17. Sheffield:Department of Biblical Studies.

Plöger, O.
1968   *Theocracy and Eschatology*. Oxford:Blackwell.

Porter, J. R.
1965   'The Legal Aspects of the Concept of "Corporate
        Personality" in the Old Testament', *VT* 15:361–80.

Rainer, R.
1984   'Crime, Law and Deviance: the Durkheim legacy',
        pp. 175–201 in *Durkheim and Modern Sociology*, ed.
        S. Fenton. Cambridge: Cambridge University Press.

Raphael, F.
1973   'Max Weber and Ancient Judaism', *Leo Baeck
        Institute Year Book* 18:41–62.

Rodd, C. S.
1979   'Max Weber and Ancient Judaism', *SJT* 32:
        457–69.
1981   'On Applying a Sociological Theory to Biblical
        Studies', *JSOT* 19:95–106.

Rogerson, J.
1970   'The Hebrew Conception of Corporate Personality',
        JTS 21:1–16.
1977   'The Old Testament View of Nature', *OTS*
        20:67–84.
1978   *Anthropology and the Old Testament*. Oxford:Blackwell.
1985   'The Use of Sociology in Old Testament Studies',
        VTS 36:245–56.
1986   'Was Early Israel a Segmentary Society?' *JSOT*
        36:17–26.

Rohrbaugh, R. L.
1978   *The Biblical Interpreter*. Philadelphia:Fortress Press.

Runciman, W. G.
1973   'What is Structuralism?' pp. 189–202 in *The
        Philosophy of Social Explanation*, ed. A. Ryan. Oxford:
        Oxford University Press.

Sasson, J. M.
1981   'On Choosing Models for Recreating Israelite Pre-
        Monarchic History', *JSOT* 21:3–24.

Schäfer-Lichtenberger, C.
1983   *Stadt und Eidgenossenschaft im Alten Testament*. BZAW
        156. Berlin:de Gruyter.

Schmueli, E.
  1968 'The "Pariah People" and its "Charismatic Leadership". A Revaluation of Max Weber's "Ancient Judaism" ', *Proceedings of the American Academy for Jewish Research* 36:167–247.
  1969 'The Novelties of the Bible and the Problem of Theodicy in Max Weber's Ancient Judaism', *JQR* 60:172–82.
Schottroff, W.
  1974 'Soziologie und Altes Testament', *VuF* 19:46–66.
  1982 'Zur Sozialgeschichte Israels in der Perserzeit', *VuF* 27:46–68.
Sigrist, C. and Neu, R.
  1988 *Ethnologische Texte zum Alten Testament. Band 1: Vor- und Frühgeschichte Israels.* Neukirchen-Vluyn: Neukirchener Verlag.
Silver, M.
  1985 *Economic Structures of the Ancient Near East.* London: Croom Helm.
Smith, M.
  1971 *Palestinian Parties and Politics that Shaped the Old Testament.* New York:Columbia University Press.
Smith, W. R.
  1927 *Lectures on the Religion of the Semites*[3]. London: A. & C. Black.
Soler, J.
  1979 'The Dietary Prohibitions of the Hebrews', *New York Review of Books* 26/10:24–30.
Stolz, F.
  1973 'Aspekte religiöser und sozialer Ordnung im alten Israel', *ZEE* 17:145–59.
Swanson, G. E.
  1964 *The Birth of the Gods.* Ann Arbor:University of Michigan.
Swingewood, A.
  1984 *A Short History of Sociological Thought.* London: Macmillan.
Theissen, G.
  1984 *Biblical Faith.* London:SCM.
Thiel, W.
  1980 *Die soziale Entwicklung Israels in vorstaatlichen Zeit.*

159

Neukirchen-Vluyn:Neukirchener Verlag.

1983 'Überlegungen zur Aufgabe einer altisraelitischen Sozialgeschichte', *Theologische Versuche* 13:11–22.

Thomas, J. J. R.

1985 'Ideology and Elective Affinity', *Sociology* 19:39–54.

Thornton, T. C. G.

1963 'Charismatic Kingship in Israel and Judah', *JTS* 14:1–11.

Tönnies, F.

1963 *Community and Society* (translated by C. P. Loomis from *Gemeinschaft und Gesellschaft* [1887]). New York: Harper & Row.

Wallis, L.

1912 *The Sociological Study of the Bible.* Chicago:University of Chicago Press.

1935 *God and the Social Process.* Chicago:University of Chicago Press.

1942 *The Bible is Human.* New York:Columbia University Press.

Weber, M.

1947 *Theory of Social and Economic Organization* (translated by A. M. Henderson and T. Parsons). New York: Free Press.

1948 *From Max Weber: Essays in Sociology* (translated by H. H. Gerth and C. Wright Mills). London: Routledge & Kegan Paul.

1949 *The Methodology of the Social Sciences* (translated and edited by E. A. Shils and H. A. Finch). New York: Free Press.

1952 *Ancient Judaism* (translated and edited by H. H. Gerth and D. Martindale from *Das antike Judentum* [1917–19]). New York:Free Press.

1954 *Max Weber on Law in Economy and Society* (translated by E. Shils and M. Rheinstein). Cambridge: Harvard University Press.

1965 *The Sociology of Religion* (translated by E. Fischoff). London:Methuen.

1968 *Economy and Society. An Outline of Interpretive Sociology* (translated by E. Fischoff *et al* from *Wirtschaft und Gesellschaft* [⁴1956]). New York:Bedminster Press.

1976 *The Protestant Ethic and the Spirit of Capitalism*[2]

(translated by T. Parsons from *Die protestantische Ethik und der Geist des Kapitalismus* [1904 – 5]). London:George Allen & Unwin.

Weisman, S.
  1977   'Charismatic Leaders in the Era of the Judges', *ZAW* 89:399 – 411.
Whitelam, K.
  1986   'Recreating the History of Israel', *JSOT* 35:45 – 70.
Williams, J. G.
  1969   'The Social Location of Israelite Prophecy', *JAAR* 37:153 – 65.
Wilson, R. R.
  1980   *Prophecy and Society*. Philadelphia:Fortress Press.
Wrong, D. H.
  1977   *Skeptical Sociology*. London:Heinemann.
Yamauchi, E.
  1984   'Sociology, Scripture and the Supernatural', *JETS* 27:169 – 92.

Abbreviations

AJS	*American Journal of Sociology*
ASR	*American Sociological Review*
BN	*Biblische Notizen*
BWANT	Beiträge zur Wissenschaft vom Alten und Neuen Testament
BZAW	Beihefte zur *Zeitschrift für die alttestamentliche Wissenschaft*
Int	*Interpretation*
JAAR	*Journal of the American Academy of Religion*
JBL	*Journal of Biblical Literature*
JBR	*Journal of Bible and Religion*
JETS	*Journal of the Evangelical Theological Society*
JNES	*Journal of Near Eastern Studies*
JQR	*Jewish Quarterly Review*
JSOT	*Journal for the Study of the Old Testament*
JTS	*Journal of Theological Studies*
MGWJ	*Monatsschrift für Geschichte und Wissenschaft des Judentums*
OTS	*Oudtestamentische Studiën*
SJT	*Scottish Journal of Theology*
ThZ	*Theologische Zeitschrift*
VT	*Vetus Testamentum*
VTS	Supplements to *Vetus Testamentum*
VuF	*Verkündigung und Forschung*
WMANT	Wissenschaftliche Monographien zum Alten und Neuen Testament
ZAW	*Zeitschrift für die alttestamentliche Wissenschaft*
ZDPV	*Zeitschrift des deutschen Palästina-Vereins*
ZEE	*Zeitschrift für evangelische Ethik*
ZRGG	*Zeitschrift für Religions- und Geistesgeschichte*

Index of Authors

Index of Subjects

165